THE WAR MANAGERS

Douglas Kinnard

AVERY PUBLISHING GROUP INC.
Wayne, New Jersey

To the

United States Army

1941–1970

"The deaths ye died
I have watched beside,
And the lives ye led
were mine."
—RUDYARD KIPLING

Cover design by Martin Hochberg and Rudy Shur
Cover photo credit: United States Army Photograph CC50481
    taken by SP5 Lawrence J. Sullivan, USA Sp Photo Det, Pac

Copyright © 1985 by Avery Publishing Group, Inc.

ISBN 0-89529-281-5

Printed in the United States of America

10 9 8 7 6 5 4 3 2

Contents

Preface

Writing late in the period of United States military intervention in the Second Indochinese War, John Kenneth Galbraith charged that "the present military generation is intimately associated with the Vietnam misfortune. And its credibility has been deeply damaged by its fatal association with the bureaucratic truths of that war—with the long succession of defeats that became victories, the victories that became defeats, and brilliant actions that did not signify anything at all."

I happened to reread that statement in the summer of 1974, about the same time I read a newspaper report that General Creighton Abrams, one of the two principal United States Commanders in Vietnam, had entered Walter Reed Army Hospital with what might well be a terminal disease. The thought occurred to me that it would be extraordinarily interesting to reassess the war from the point of view of its Army General Officer managers while they were still available and before their memories of the war faded.

What was the view of those against whom in large part Galbraith made his charge? Would it be a uniform view, a mind-set to the effect that the civilian leadership and the public had let the expeditionary force down, as one sometimes heard, or would there be some useful introspection about the way the war had been fought? These questions set me off in September 1974 on the study from which this book has resulted.

That there is a need for reassessments of the Vietnam War is self-evident. The potentially profound consequences of the war on United States foreign policy for years to come appear in themselves to require a look into the various facets of the conflict, and as soon as possible. It is important that we understand all we can about that disaster, for the benefit of politicians, bureaucrats, military leaders, diplomats, newsmen, scholars, and the interested public. Not all agree: in a much-quoted statement, Samuel P. Huntington asserted that it is "conceivable that our policy-makers may best meet future crises and dilemmas if they simply blot out of their minds any recollection of this one." At the 1968 conference where that remark was made, he was supported by Albert Wohlstetter but countered by a number of other participants.

Now that the divisive issue has ended, there is an impulse to forget it, but unfortunately the war will not go away. We owe it to ourselves and future policy-makers to get a better grasp on what went wrong. For one thing, the war should be a lesson that will help us to understand better in the future the problems and limitations of applying force to influence world events. Clearly, many of our difficulties in Vietnam were of our own making. We should learn to know ourselves better—both our strengths and our weaknesses. Moreover, even the severest critics of the war may benefit from new insights on what caused the gap between the results achieved and the astonishingly high expenditure of men and resources.

In reassessing the Vietnam experience, one must come to grips with the role of the senior military. Barbara Tuchman tells us that the war was not some aberration of the generals, but "a product of civilian policy shaped by three successive civilian Presidents and their academic and other civilian advisers." Similarly, it has been maintained that no expeditionary force has ever been subjected to so many detailed constraints upon the military commanders' freedom of action, and at the same time received such severe criticism for not achieving better results. On another level, however, there are allegations that the manner in which the war was conducted militarily, such as in the massive employment of firepower, was politically counterproductive. And on still another level, it is alleged that the military did not adapt themselves to the Vietnamese environment—that they fought the war along the lines in which they had been trained to perform in more familiar environments. In any case, it is probably true that the manner in which policy from Washington was perceived and implemented in Vietnam in turn conditioned subsequent policy from Washington.

There are millions of words in print concerning such issues, but more is needed from the field officers who were conducting the war. The Pentagon Papers are highly useful but must be used cautiously. As their title implies, they largely show the view from the Pentagon and Washington sides, not from Vietnam itself; and significant documentation has been left out because it was not available. Undoubtedly the operational experiences of the authors in Vietnam affected the papers, but none was an operational commander at the general officer level.

My purpose is limited but important: to tell the story of the Second Indochinese War from the perspectives of the United States Army General Officers who commanded there. This is not a history, nor is it a personal memoir; it is an attempt to record and analyze the retrospective views of the men who managed the operational aspects of the war. The inquiry is pragmatic—it draws together the issues and opinions of these war managers. In the end no one can speak for the group, but they have spoken for themselves and enable me to present what appear to be their views.

In September 1974, when the final outcome of the war was still unknown, I mailed a sixty-item questionnaire to the 173 Army Generals who had commanded in Vietnam. The response was astonishing—64 percent of them completed the questionnaire, and many added pages of comment. It was evident, however, that additional research was necessary to place the issues in their proper perspective. There were available to me the usual secondary sources and published government documents, as well as the highly unusual Pentagon Papers. In addition, I was able to do research in certain files in the Army Center of Military History and conduct in-depth interviews with a selected group of the generals who responded to the questionnaires.

A number of persons have been of great assistance to me. First of all, there are the generals themselves (most of whom wish to remain anonymous), who took the time to answer the questionnaire; certain of them also granted interviews. My colleague at the University of Vermont, Professor Peter Grabosky, helped greatly in the initial analysis of the data. Vincent Demma of the Army Center of Military History was of great assistance in helping me find my way through what are still, understandably, working files for the Army historians. Too many others to mention individually were also helpful. In the end, however, the judgment was mine as to what material should be used and what conclusions to draw from it.

Burlington, Vermont   Douglas Kinnard
                                                        Brigadier General
                                                        United States Army (Ret.)

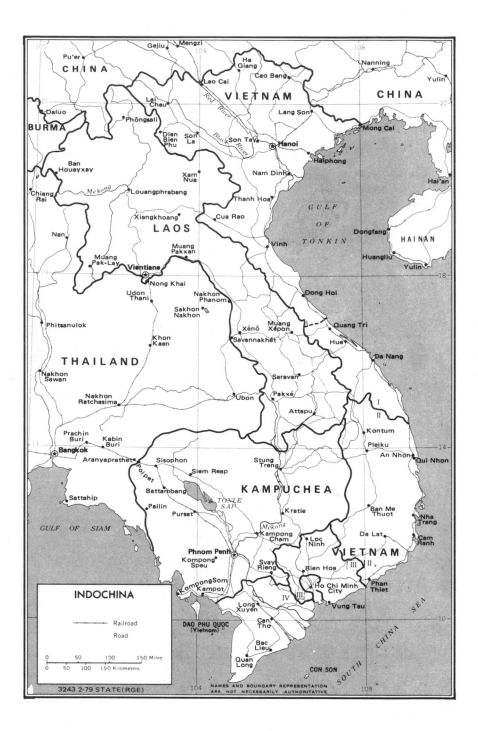

INDOCHINA

Railroad
Road

| 0 | 50 | 100 | 150 Miles |
| 0 | 50 | 100 | 150 Kilometers |

3243 2-79 STATE(RGE)

NAMES AND BOUNDARY REPRESENTATION
ARE NOT NECESSARILY AUTHORITATIVE

The War Managers

 # Introduction

To have once been part of the tragedy lent a special poignancy for me to events in South Vietnam in the spring of 1975.[1] On the television news were the familiar background scenes, but now the action was turned around, as though 1965 were being replayed but without the American intervention.

The year had started quietly in South Vietnam with the expectation that there would be no general offensive in 1975 by the North Vietnamese, but rather a series of probing attacks leading to an all-out effort in 1976. However, in mid-January the provincial capital of Phuoc Long, one of the eleven provinces in Military Region III surrounding Saigon, fell to the Communists. That was hardly reassuring, but not in itself critical.

In March the action that had been gradually building up began in earnest. Communist forces attacked along an immense area running down Route 14, a strategic inland road extending from the Central Highlands city of Pleiku all the way to Tay Ninh city northwest of Saigon.

Obviously such an attack was a major violation of the Paris peace agreement of two years earlier. The reaction of the United States was predictable. Congressional acts in 1973 had made any United States military intervention virtually impossible. The reaction of a Congressional mission just returning from Vietnam, together with public opinion in general, made it highly doubtful that any of the increased military aid that the Ford Administration was requesting would be forthcoming.

1. I had two tours of duty in Vietnam: in 1966–67 as a Colonel, I was Chief of Operations Analysis in J-3 of the Military Assistance Command. In 1969–70 I was Commanding General of II Field Force Artillery and subsequently Chief of Staff of the II Field Force Vietnam (a Corps-sized Force).

The beginning of the collapse itself was the capture of Ban Me Thuot, a remote provincial capital on Highway 14. At this point President Nguyen Van Thieu made a critical decision that caught everyone by surprise, including United States officials in Saigon and Washington. He ordered the withdrawal of South Vietnamese forces from the highlands to the coast—the most difficult of all military maneuvers. The Army of South Vietnam had never been trained for a war of maneuver in the traditional sense. The outcome of this withdrawal was a military disaster.

At the same time, the North Vietnamese began pressure in the north near the Hue area, where after some vacillation the South Vietnamese regional commanding general, Ngo Quang Truong, ordered a withdrawal. Another disaster. This time panic ensued as tens of thousands of civilians crowded the roads, communications were lost, and military units simply disintegrated. A South Vietnamese official was quoted as saying at the time: "Pleiku *fini*, Kontum *fini*, Ban Me Thuot *fini*, Hue *fini*. Everything *fini*." So it was.

It was impossible to organize a defense. Some South Vietnamese forces fought well—the 18th Division at Xuan Loc east of Saigon comes to mind—but by April it was clear that there was no chance of success. The events of March and twenty years of struggle were too much; morale was broken, and the end of the Republic of Vietnam was at hand. To be sure, as late as the middle of April, Army Chief of Staff Frederick Weyand, an old Vietnamese hand, was still talking to Congress about aid—but the charade was over. Officially it ended on April 30, only hours after the last Americans were helicoptered off the United States Embassy roof, when the flag of the Provisional Revolutionary Government was raised in Saigon.

The Nixon illusion of Vietnamization had been shattered. Obviously we had deluded ourselves about the military capability of South Vietnam. Secretary of Defense James Schlesinger was quoted as saying: "It is obvious in retrospect that the strength, resiliency, and steadfastness of the Saigon forces were more highly valued than they should have been." The light at the end of the tunnel had been reached, and it was red.

The origins of the United States involvement that ended in the disastrous spring of 1975 began in World War II. There seems ample evidence of Franklin Roosevelt's opposition to a French return to Indo-China at the end of the war—perhaps through some kind of international trusteeship when the Japanese occupiers were defeated. Nevertheless, in the interest of the ongoing war, the President was reluctant to get into operational details until the struggle with the Axis was concluded.

In the months following Truman's assumption of the Presidency in April 1945, the policy seems to have been not to assist the French to reestablish control of Indo-China, but rather to watch in order to determine whether the French had the support of the indigenous population. The trusteeship plan appears to have been abandoned in the interest of United States relationships with the French government.

By the time fighting broke out between the French and the Vietnamese in 1946, the problem of the defeat of the Axis powers had been replaced by the perceived problem of the Soviet threat to Western Europe. In effect the Vietnam problem was subsumed within a larger international context, and this time one in which it was to remain—the Cold War. At the outset the notion of eventual self-government for the Indochinese was maintained, but as the Cold War hardened in the late 1940's, such aspirations for the Vietnamese were lost in the maze of the containment policy.

In early 1950 France made an appeal to the United States for direct military aid in Indo-China because of the drain that the war against the Vietminh was placing on French resources. Up to that point the United States had refrained from supplying military equipment directly to Indo-China, but from the spring of 1950 on, this policy was abandoned and an incremental involvement of the United States began.

The major change came with the North Korean invasion of South Korea in June 1950, from which point on Indo-China became solidly an element of defense against the perceived Sino-Soviet plan to dominate the free world. As President Truman said later in his memoirs: "We were seeing a pattern in Indo-China timed to coincide with the attack in Korea as a challenge to the Western World."

This notion of a worldwide Communist effort was subsequently accepted by both Dwight Eisenhower and John Kennedy. For his part, President Eisenhower took over from the French after the 1954 Geneva Accords, with a substantial advisory and training effort for the South Vietnamese forces. The United States commitment was not large by later standards, involving only about 700 advisers and the expenditure of about $200 million in military aid by the time his administration ended in 1961. Eisenhower also popularized the domino theory that Dean Acheson had put forth in 1950 in somewhat different terms.

Escalation by the Kennedy Administration was substantial. When President Kennedy was assassinated, there were approximately 16,000 United States troops in South Vietnam, including Special Forces. The brunt of American involvement in Vietnam fell, however, on the Johnson and Nixon administrations, and it is with the period from the introduction of United States fighting forces in 1965 until their withdrawal in early 1973 that this book is mainly concerned.

The period of massive United States military involvement peaked in the spring of 1969 at almost 550,000 military personnel. A substantial part of that force was the Army, arrayed in a combat and advisory role up and down the length of Vietnam. This army force was commanded by some 183 Army General Officers, from one to four stars in rank and in commands all the way from Generals William Westmoreland and Creighton Abrams to one-star generals who controlled anywhere from 5,000 troops upward. These were the individuals who in the final analysis bore the responsibility for the conduct of the Army's war in Vietnam. They were, to borrow a phrase, Westmoreland's Lieutenants. What follows is as much as possible their story, their retrospective view of the war in Vietnam when the outcome was still uncertain, before the debacle in the spring of 1975.

A substantial number of allegations have been made concerning the general-officer managers of the Vietnamese War, and we should look at those charges before discussing the generals themselves.

Perhaps the greatest body of critical commentary concerns the manner in which this group perceived and fought the war. The overall criticism is that the military leadership failed to understand the revolutionary character of the war. Specifically, it is said that the military approached Vietnam as it did World War II and Korea and neglected to appreciate the political side of the conflict or the fact that it was a revolution, involving many aspects of Vietnamese society. As a corollary of this limited view, there was, it is claimed, no anticipation of the harmful side effects of United States strategies and programs on Vietnamese society. Frequently cited as supporting evidence is a statement by Chairman of the Joint Chiefs Earle G. Wheeler: "It is fashionable in some quarters to say that the problems in Southeast Asia are primarily political and economic rather than Military. I do not agree. The essence of the problem in Vietnam is military."[2]

One of the most trenchant critiques of the manner in which the American military perceived and fought the war was written by Sir Robert Thompson, who had been earlier involved in the British struggle in Malaysia and was for four years with the British advisory mission in Vietnam. In effect, his judgment is that the American military leadership, failing to understand the nature of the war, failed to adopt the correct counterstrategy toward the Vietcong and North Vietnamese, who for their part succeeded in making the war a test of will rather than of strength.[3]

Henry Kissinger, writing in *Foreign Affairs* just before joining the Nixon administration, also took the military leadership to task for its performance in Vietnam, especially for its objective of destroying enemy troops rather than protecting the friendly population—although it is not clear from the article how he would have accomplished the one without the other.[4]

One more critique by an insider, Colonel Donald Bletz, may be sufficient. Bletz, too, concludes that the military did a good job in Vietnam on the technical level but was unable to come to grips with the politicomilitary aspects of the war. Specifically, he feels that the application of force was so all-pervasive that it was frequently inconsistent with the political objective. The military profession, he says, "was faced with a new and unprecedented challenge and it failed to meet that challenge fully."[5]

A second area of critical commentary concerns the manner in which progress in the war was measured and reported. Since the war was nonlinear (there were no front lines), some method of measuring progress had to be designed to replace the lines on a map. What was developed was a series of statistical indicators that

2. Quoted in Henry Brandon, *Anatomy of Error* (Boston, Gambit, 1969), p. 23.

3. Thompson, *No Exit from Vietnam* (New York, David McKay, 1970), especially pp. 63–64.

4. Henry Kissinger, "The Vietnam Negotiations," *Foreign Affairs*, 47 (January 1969), 211–234. The Kissinger critique and others are expertly woven together by Bernard Brodie in his usual superb style in *War and Politics* (New York, Macmillan, 1973), chap. 5.

5. Bletz, *The Role of the Military in U.S. Foreign Policy* (New York, Praeger, 1972), pp. 278, 279, 281.

have been subject to criticism on at least three levels. First, the techniques were crude and the operators of the system lacked the actual operational experience to employ such techniques in a meaningful and sophisticated way. Second, the military are by nature committed to success, hence any statistical reporting system was bound to be on the optimistic side and distorted when ultimately viewed by officials in Washington. Third, such reports had an enormous impact on national policy with regard to the conduct of the war.[6] The fourth criticism has to do with the "body count," which, since the war objectives were heavily weighted toward attriting the enemy, was a basic element of the reporting system. Critics contend that the reports were often exaggerated, frequently for reasons of careerism—since a high body count was the mark of an effective command—and further, that many of the bodies were Vietnamese civilians, killed indiscriminately.[7]

The manner in which the military shaped the Army of South Vietnam (ARVN) has also received considerable critical commentary. Basically, the charge is one of mirror-imaging: the United States created an army similar to its own—designed, at least as structured, to fight wars in Europe or of the Korean type. Furthermore, such an army could not long be supported by the Republic on its own and in any case was not the proper instrument for fighting a counterguerrilla war. Rather, it is stated, ARVN units should have been smaller and less dependent on heavy firepower or helicopter support of the United States type. The commentary was made before the final collapse of South Vietnam—a collapse that ironically was brought about by a very conventional war indeed, but a war of movement for which the South Vietnamese had not been trained.

Another group of criticisms of the American military leadership in Vietnam has to do with what may be broadly described as professionalism and careerism—meaning stress on creating a performance image rather than on achieving positive results, or using the war for one's own ends, or not asking the critical questions. One of the more unusual commentators on this issue was retired Marine General David Shoup, who implies that many of the generals and

6. Brodie, pp. 194, 195.
7. One of the more critical discussions of the body count is in Edward L. King, *The Death of the Army* (New York, Saturday Review Press, 1972), pp. 101, 105, 106.

admirals were anxious to get the United States more deeply involved in the war in order to practice and enhance their own careers.[8] Another variant of this criticism concerns the military mind, sometimes equated with the bureaucratic mind. In a June 1969 meeting at the Adlai Stevenson Institute, Henry Kissinger ascribed such a mind to General William C. Westmoreland, who at that point was just relinquishing his command in Vietnam.[9]

Other commentary along these lines castigates particular subgroups of the officer corps for not being more professionally critical of the conduct of the war. Perhaps, one author speculates, the course of that war would have been different if the West Pointers at the higher levels had asked more critical questions—thus indicating that West Pointers were so imbued with the notion of following orders that they were not likely to question either the manner in which the war was being conducted or the basic premises of United States strategy.[10] One also hears occasionally of the young-old dichotomy, wherein the younger officers were critical of their seniors for waging a war of big units maneuvering all over South Vietnam rather than concentrating on the political and economic problems of that country.[11]

A final cluster of critical commentary concerning the war managers deals with the general area of military-civilian conflict over the conduct of the war. Within the military, the conflict manifested itself as a conviction that the military was the victim of poor civilian policies, such as the incremental approach to escalating the employment of force pursued by Defense Secretary Robert S. McNamara. According to this view, the military see themselves as scapegoats for the war.[12] Elsewhere one can find the opposite

8. Shoup, "The New American Militarism," *Atlantic Monthly* (April 1969), pp. 51–56. See also William R. Corson, *Consequences of Failure* (New York, Norton, 1974), p. 104.

9. Richard M. Pfeffer, ed., *No More Vietnams?* (New York, Harper, 1968), pp. 11, 12.

10. J. Arthur Hiese, *The Brass Factories* (Washington, Public Affairs Press, 1969), pp. 163, 164.

11. See, for example, an article by Ted Sell in the *Washington Post* entitled "Younger Military Critics of Viet Policy Emerging into Positions of Power," (March 25, 1968), p. A15.

12. Ward Just, *Military Men* (New York, Knopf, 1970). Stephen E. Ambrose and James A. Barber, Jr., *The Military and American Society* (New York, Free Press, 1972). Bletz, *Role of the Military*.

view—that senior military professionals misled the civilian leadership through incompetence or unwillingness to speak up.[13]

I began to study the war from the perspective of its general-officer managers in September 1974, before the outcome of the war was known, by mailing a sixty-item questionnaire to each of the 173 Army General Officers who had held command positions in Vietnam during 1965–72.[14] The generals were more or less aware of the criticism I have summarized above, although the questionnaire itself did not explicitly raise it. Respondents were promised anonymity, and questionnaire items were limited to matters bearing directly on the Vietnam War. Furthermore, the questions concentrated on aspects of the war on which members of this group had had first-hand knowledge or had a sound professional basis for opinion.

The areas covered included clarity, understanding, and realism of the United States objectives; fighting the war—that is, tactics employed, command and control of the war effort, and interservice cooperation; measuring the results that were being achieved; the drive to improve the South Vietnamese Army; the pacification program; the professionalism of the United States Army Officer Corps; the rules of engagement; media coverage of the war; the overall outcome of the war; and recommended changes in the foregoing areas if it had to be done over again.

Despite having been a general in Vietnam myself and knowing many of the group personally, the response of 67 percent, with 64 percent returning completed questionnaires, constitutes an extraordinarily high level of cooperation, given the nature of the survey and its subjects. Respondents were invited to append marginal

13. Shoup, "The New American Militarism." Townsend Hoopes, *The Limits of Intervention* (New York, David McKay, 1969). Chester L. Cooper, *the Lost Crusade* (New York, Dodd, Mead, 1970). Daniel Ellsberg, *Papers on the War* (New York, Simon and Schuster, 1972).

14. There were 183 individuals. At the time of the mailing, however, nine were deceased, and I excluded myself from the survey. General Officer command positions charged with the operational management of the war in Vietnam were: Commander, U.S. Military Assistance Command Vietnam (COMUSMACV); Deputy COMUSMACV; Chief of Staff USMACV; Commanding General (CG), Field Force or U.S. Corps; Chief of Staff Field Force or U.S. Corps; CG Artillery, Field Force or U.S. Corps; Division Commander; Assistant Division Commander; GC Separate Brigade; Advisor Vietnamese Corps or equivalent position.

notations and narrative comments. Many did so, some writing many pages. The data will be used throughout the book, along with other research data obtained in interviews with selected principals and materials obtained by normal research means.

These war managers were born between 1910 and 1926, with the median at 1918; therefore when Franklin Roosevelt took office in 1933 at the height of the Great Depression, the majority were in high school or grade school. General William Westmoreland, at the older end of the group, was a plebe at West Point in 1933.

Most of the group received their commissions as second lieutenants during or just before World War II, and a large percentage saw action in that war. Fewer than half were in combat during the Korean War of 1950–3. West Point produced approximately half, and of the remainder, most were integrated into the Regular Army just after World War II, on the basis of their service in that war. Almost all were college graduates, but relatively few were from elite universities.

As for branch of service, over 60 percent had been infantry; of the remainder, there were more former Artillery officers than Armor.[15] About half of the generals were Airborne qualified, and at the time of the survey (September 1974) about half of the group had retired from the Army.

Length of tours in Vietnam for this group varied from one to fifty-five months, the median being one year. A substantial minority held more than one general officer position. These positions were spread throughout the country, relatively few being in the Delta. The III Corps Tactical Zone, which comprised the eleven provinces around Saigon, was substantially better represented than either of the two Corps Tactical Zones to the North. Vietnam service brought some upward mobility to the generals: the average rank in Vietnam of one and a half stars went to two stars for the group by September 1974.

What answers to the questionnaire could be expected by members of this group? Judging by the literature on military elites, we should be able to group the responses into seven categories. We will return to them briefly in Chapter 7 and in detail in Appendix II.

(1) *Respondents will manifest some dissatisfaction with aspects of the war which were under Washington's managerial control.* A

15. Technically, once promoted to general, an officer no longer has a branch of service.

familiar theme in the literature on the war concerned the views of senior military personnel toward the management of the war by civilians in the White House and the Pentagon. A number of observers with academic, journalistic, or public service backgrounds have made reference to restraints imposed on theater-level operations by Washington managers, and to the attendant frustrations experienced by high-ranking officers in Vietnam.[16]

(2) *Respondents will be generally satisfied with those aspects of the war which were under the managerial control of the United States Army personnel at the theater level.* The existing literature on elites suggests that members of such a group tend to manifest attitudes that might best be characterized as self-protective.

Writings by generals on the outcome of operations undertaken by United States forces throughout the war were generally favorable. While military managers might have regarded the restraints imposed upon them from Washington with some discomfort, available materials suggest that they were generally pleased with aspects of the war over which they exercised independent control. It was in the area of theater-level operations that the generals assumed direct responsibility; where praise or blame is to be accorded the military managers themselves, one would expect a tendency to accentuate the positive. In other words, although the respondents did not enjoy the resources and latitude they might have desired, they could be expected to express satisfaction with the execution of field-level efforts.

(3) *Respondents will express satisfaction with and pride in the professionalism of United States Army personnel.* The justification for this hypothesis is similar to that which has been offered in support of the proposition concerning attitudes toward theater-level management. Pride in performance has been a traditional characteristic of members of the American military. Aside from the grim events surrounding the My Lai massacre, generals would be likely to suggest that United States Army officers as a whole conducted themselves in a highly professional manner.

(4) *Respondents will be generally pessimistic with regard to the capabilities of ARVN to defend against Viet Cong and North Viet-*

16. Morris Janowitz, *The Professional Soldier* (New York, Free Press, 1960, 1971), p. xxiii. Sam C. Sarkesian, *The Professional Army Officer in a Changing Society* (Chicago, Nelson-Hall, 1975), pp. 189–190. Brodie, p. 180. Maureen Mylander, *The Generals* (New York, Dial Press, 1974), pp. 209, 220.

namese forces. The inadequacy of South Vietnamese forces was a recurring theme in journalistic reporting and other writings in the years prior to the implementation of the Vietnamization program. Maxwell Taylor has spoken of the frustrations caused him by the political intrigue with which high-ranking members of the South Vietnamese military were preoccupied during his tenure as Ambassador.[17] Throughout the 1960's, ARVN forces were plagued with high desertion rates and a significant amount of poor leadership. Frances Fitzgerald's account of ARVN corruption and ineptitude is, if not fully documented, at least grimly illustrative.[18]

(5) *Respondents will harbor negative views concerning coverage of the war by newspaper and television journalists*. A unique aspect of the Second Indo-Chinese War was the extent and immediacy of its coverage by the news media, and the fact that this was the first televised war in American history was even more important in view of the divisions that emerged within American society.

News stories critical of policies and practices in Vietnam were the subject of attack from various levels of management, from the White House down to the combat theater.[19] Indeed, some critics of the media maintained that press coverage was of significant assistance to the enemy. It thus appeared likely that, given the extent of antiwar sentiment in the press corps and eventually in the public at large, the generals' views of press coverage would be less than positive.

(6) *Respondents will express some dissatisfaction with the overall results of the United States efforts*. Even the most supportive observers of United States activity in Southeast Asia in September 1974 were reluctant to view the Vietnam War as an unqualified success. The result of United States efforts was not, even before the final outcome was known, a victory in the normal sense. At the time of the cease fire the Vietcong and North Vietnamese presence in the South was salient, to say the least; by the time the survey was administered, twenty months later, that presence had become

17. Maxwell D. Taylor, *Swords and Plowshares* (New York, Norton, 1972), p. 330.

18. Frances Fitzgerald, *Fire in the Lake* (Boston, Little Brown, 1972), pp. 314–315. See also David Halberstam, *The Best and the Brightest* (New York, Random House, 1972), pp. 318, 336, 413, 542, 567, 582.

19. See, for example, Senator Clifford P. Hansen's criticism of bias in media coverage of the Vietnam War, 92nd Congress, 1st Session, *Congressional Record*, Vol. 117, pp. 6310–11.

even more threatening. This contrasts markedly with the aftermath of the only other recent limited war in which the United States had been involved—the Korean War.

Moreover, the objectives of United States involvement were narrowed during the period 1965–72; the more ambitious goal of defeating the enemy forces was revised to that of providing the South Vietnamese with the training and material resources necessary to continue the war themselves at whatever level the enemy might elect. This aspirational retrenchment, the result of increasing domestic antipathy toward the war effort along with unprecedented criticism of United States military institutions, might be expected to lead major participants to view the overall outcome in a less than favorable light.

(7) *Respondents will manifest a strong consensus in each of the substantive areas covered.*

The basis for predicting a strong consensus rests primarily on the overwhelming homogeneity of the respondents. Individuals returning completed questionnaires were, without exception, white males drawn from the combat branches of the United States Army; with one exception, all were married. A substantial majority of the respondents were Protestant, and, as noted, all were born during the period 1910–26. The most significant dimension, of course, was common professional experience. Each respondent had experienced at least a quarter-century of successful passage upward through the Army hierarchy, surviving a standard series of rigorous screening procedures. Each had experienced previous combat in World War II and/or Korea; each had attended the United States Army Command and General Staff College and one of the War Colleges. Moreover, the tour of each man serving as a general officer in Vietnam was personally approved by Generals Westmoreland or Abrams. It also seemed likely that the nature of the questionnaire itself would tend to produce a consensus among respondents, for the questions concerned specialized phenomena that were tightly bound together in time and space.

War for What Objectives?

After the war was over, in the summer of 1975, I visited with General Matthew Ridgway in his home in the Fox Chapel section of Pittsburgh. When the discussion reached the war in Vietnam, he said that he never really had been sure of what General Westmoreland's objectives were in Vietnam and told me the following anecdote. Shortly after Tet 1968, President Johnson had asked Ridgway to the White House to discuss the Vietnam situation. In the course of a two-hour meeting, there were numerous interruptions by telephone calls to Johnson and by Johnson's aides. During one of these interruptions, Ridgway turned to Vice President Humphrey, his companion in the visit with LBJ, and said that he had "never known what General Westmoreland's mission was." Humphrey replied, "That's a good question, General. Ask the President when he gets off the phone."[1] Ridgway and Humphrey were not the only ones uncertain about the objectives in Vietnam.

Before the outbreak of the Korean War, two National Security Council (NSC) papers had set the terms for the overall United States objectives with respect to Indo-China. They were intended to set forth what later became known as the "domino principle."[2] The special importance of Indo-China was related to the fact that it was the only area in which a large European army (French) was in conflict with "communists" (Viet Minh). The key operative paragraphs are:

1. Halberstam cites the same story in *The Best and the Brightest*, p. 145.

2. References to the *Pentagon Papers (PP)* refer to the Gravel Edition and will simply show the volume and page numbers after the abbreviation *PP*. In this case: NSC 48/2 (December 1949) and NSC 64 (February 1950), *PP*, Vol. 1, pp. 82, 83.

It is important to United States security interests that all
practicable measures be taken to prevent further communist
expansion in Southeast Asia. Indo-China is a key area of
Southeast Asia and is under immediate threat.

The neighboring countries of Thailand and Burma could be
expected to fall under Communist domination if Indo-China
were controlled by a Communist-dominated government.
The balance of Southeast Asia would then be in grave hazard.

The outbreak of the Korean War in 1950, and particularly the
Chinese intervention that fall, had the effect on United States
policymakers of making the French struggle in Indo-China appear
as part of the world-wide struggle to contain communism. At this
point the People's Republic of China rather than the Soviet Union
was perceived as the principal source of the Communist threat to
Southeast Asia.[3]

By the time Dien Bien Phu fell in May 1954, the United States
was paying 80 percent of the cost of the French effort in Indo-
China. In October President Eisenhower informed Premier Diem
(who became chief of state the following October) that henceforth
United States aid would be given directly to his government rather
than through the French.[4] In a few months a United States Military Assistance Group was on the ground to take over from the
French the training of South Vietnamese armed forces.

During the Eisenhower years, the commitment of advisers was
not large numerically, never reaching 1,000 personnel. As the Viet
Cong insurgent activity, which surfaced by 1957, began to reach
serious proportions in 1959, however, the United States objectives
changed: not only were the South Vietnamese to be assisted in
building up their forces to assure internal security, but they were
to be encouraged to plan a defense against external aggression.

This was the situation when Kennedy took office in January 1961.
In view of what was perceived as a steadily deteriorating situation,
the new President in May dispatched the Vice President to meet

3. NSC 124/2, *PP*, 1: 384–390.
4. The previous month, September 1954, the Southeast Asia Collective Treaty had been signed, and South Vietnam became eligible for both
the protective features and the economic benefits that the Treaty provided. (The Geneva Agreement in July which negotiated the French ar-
mistice, had temporarily divided the country at the 17th parallel into a
North and South Vietnam.)

with Diem. The outcome of LBJ's visit was a new Presidential program for South Vietnam, announced in May and designed to strengthen the Diem government, as well as to improve its popular support in that country and in the United States. Major military changes included increasing the aid program, increasing the regular SVN forces to 200,000, and providing United States Special Forces to train the South Vietnamese. A decision not announced at the time was to study the possible commitment of United States forces at some time in the future.

In October 1961 the famous Taylor-Rostow investigation of the situation in South Vietnam took place. Following the Taylor recommendations, President Kennedy sent in additional advisers, equipment, and support, including helicopter units, although he did not approve the introduction of a United States military task force, as Taylor had also recommended. By the following spring United States advisers had increased to over 5,000. The Taylor mission was a definite benchmark in the escalation of the war but did not change United States objectives in a formal sense.

In 1962 President Kennedy announced another increase in United States military assistance within the overall objective of preventing a communist South Vietnam and building a peaceful and free society. By May 1963 there were 12,000 advisers in Vietnam. In that same month the police handling of riots in Hue set off disputes between the Buddhists and the Vietnamese Government. The handling of these disputes caused increasing concern within the United States Government over the viability of the Diem regime. This feeling of disenchantment was expressed publicly by President Kennedy in a television interview in September 1963, but in the same week the President indicated his opposition to reducing aid for the GVN. The threat of China to Southeast Asia was cited by him as central to the problem.

By November the United States had a new ambassador on station in Saigon, Henry Cabot Lodge, and the United States troop level was at 16,500. In that same month Diem and Kennedy were assassinated, and the new United States President affirmed American support for South Vietnam. United States objectives were not noticeably changed. They included assisting the GVN to defeat the externally controlled Communist conspiracy and to develop and maintain public support in the south.[5]

5. NSAM 273, *PP*, 3: 17–19.

Whatever ambiguity there may have been in the degree of commitment of the United States up to this point, none was left after publication of NSAM 288 in March 1964:

> We seek an independent non-Communist South Vietnam.
> We do not require that it serve as a Western base or as a
> member of a Western alliance. South Vietnam must be free,
> however, to accept outside assistance as required to maintain
> its security. This assistance should be able to take the form not
> only of economic and social measures but also police and mili-
> tary help to root out and control insurgent elements. [6]

That spring Robert McNamara made one of his many visits to South Vietnam and met with the incoming and outgoing United States Commanders, Generals William Westmoreland and Paul Harkins. "Paul," asked McNamara, "how long do you think it will take to wind up this war?" Harkins responded, "Oh, I think we can change the tide in about six months." Westmoreland said later that he found this exchange incredible. [7]

In part as a result of McNamara's trip, the report, which was not encouraging, moved President Johnson to ask Lodge and Westmoreland to meet with his principal Washington advisers in Honolulu. Westmoreland and Lodge played major roles in the con-ference, but the outcome was that there was no change in objec-tives. At this point the Republican Convention was only a few weeks away, and LBJ was not interested in setting up any barn-sized targets. He even resurrected a letter from President Eisenhower to Diem in 1954 and implied that the letter still set forth the basic American position.

In July a new Ambassador, Maxwell Davenport Taylor, arrived in Saigon to replace Lodge. Taylor, a graduate of West Point, was an impressive-looking officer, urbane and a good speaker, with the reputation of being something of an intellectual. He had risen in prominence within the Army in the latter part of World War II,

6. *PP*, 2: 412.
7. Considerable information from this point on in the present book was obtained by me from annotations on the questionnaires and from in-depth interviews of principals. In most cases the generals asked to remain anonymous. At times I will quote verbatim and so indicate with quotation marks; at other times I will paraphrase. Westmoreland tells this story in slightly different words in his *A Soldier Reports* (New York, Doubleday, 1976), p. 67.

and, as those things sometimes happen, the conventional wisdom in the Army seemed to point to his eventual appointment as Chief of Staff. Eisenhower did appoint him to that job, but it was a frustrating four years for Taylor. He attempted to sell Eisenhower a strategy less dependent on nuclear arms than the one the President had selected for budgetary reasons. Taylor called his strategy "flexible response," but Eisenhower would have none of it.

When he retired in 1959, Taylor wrote *The Uncertain Trumpet*, in which he told of his attempts to gain acceptance for his strategy. In the 1960 campaign Kennedy used Taylor's ideas, which became central to the Kennedy defense platform. In the wake of the Bay of Pigs fiasco, Kennedy returned Taylor to government, first as his military adviser and subsequently as Chairman of the Joint Chiefs of Staff. Now he was in Vietnam as ambassador. That Taylor was one of the chief architects of the United States intervention in Vietnam there is little doubt, although he showed ambivalence at times about the United States troop commitment.

Shortly after he arrived in Vietnam as ambassador, Taylor held a staff meeting at which he set forth his views on United States objectives in that country. His approach was based upon a paper evidently prepared in Washington prior to his departure. The new commander of the Military Assistance Command, William Westmoreland, was in the audience. One member of the audience interpreted the basic objectives to be: achieving political stability in South Vietnam; preventing the enemy from taking over the country; and preparing the GVN for a counteroffensive against the Vietcong. Taylor went on to touch on some other considerations.

> The Sino-Soviet bloc is watching attentively the course of events in South Vietnam to see whether subversive insurgency is indeed the form which the "wave of the future" will take.
>
> Failure in Southeast Asia would destroy U.S. influence throughout Asia and severely damage our standing elsewhere throughout the world. It would be the prelude to the loss or neutralization of all of Southeast Asia and the absorption of that area into the Chinese empire.

During the early afternoon of August 4, 1964, the United States destroyers *Maddox* and *C. Turner Joy* were apparently subjected to an attack by some torpedo boats of the North Vietnamese Navy. The *Maddox* had been similarly attacked two days previously. The precise nature of the destroyers' mission and the exact location of the attack with respect to the coastline of North Vietnam have been subjects of controversy ever since. On the night of August 4, President Johnson informed the nation of the second attack, indicating that air action was in progress against NVN gunboats and supporting facilities and that he would seek a Congressional resolution making it clear that the United States was united in its efforts in Southeast Asia.

Subsequently, in his request to Congress for the resolution, Johnson linked the objectives of his administration in Southeast Asia with those of Eisenhower and Kennedy. On August 10 Congress passed Public Law 88-409, the so-called Tonkin Gulf Resolution, by a margin of 502 to 2 votes. The resolution declared that Congress supported the determination of the President to take all necessary measures to prevent further aggression and added: "The United States regards as vital to its national interest and to world peace the maintenance of national peace and security in Southeast Asia. . . ." Furthermore, the United States was prepared "to take all necessary steps, including the use of armed force, to assist any member or protocol state of the Southeast Asia collective defense treaty."

During the middle of August Westmoreland sent a message to Washington in which he suggested that consideration be given to improving the military posture in South Vietnam: he advocated sending quick-reaction Marine forces to Da Nang and an Army brigade to Tan Son Nhut airfield near Saigon. Ambassador Taylor was not interested at the moment in this sort of commitment, and with the presidential campaign underway the proposal, for the time being at least, got nowhere.

In mid-September a message came from Secretary of State Dean Rusk to the Ambassador which expressed the full commitment of the United States to the security of South Vietnam, and in stronger terms than heretofore. In that same month Saigon formed its third government since Diem—an unhappy experience for the United States, which was looking for stability in Saigon. That was "probably the last opportunity for the United States to have washed its hands of South Vietnam," Westmoreland was to say in his memoirs.

Westmoreland in that fall of 1964 was something to behold. First Captain of his West Point class, his career as an officer was like something out of the *Army Career Management Manual*. Maxwell Taylor, who first met "Westy" in Sicily in World War II when the younger officer was seven years out of West Point, wrote later: "His sure-handed manner of command led to the entry of his name in a little black book I carried to record the names of exceptional young officers for future reference."[8] After the war Westmoreland left the Field Artillery to become an infantryman parachutist, and by the last year of the Korean War he was a young Brigadier commanding the 187th Regimental Combat Team in combat. After a short stay at the Harvard Business School, he became Secretary of the Army General Staff, and in 1957 he was the youngest Major General in the Army. Thereafter came command of an Airborne Division, the Superintendency of West Point, and command of the Army's Airborne Corps. After Harkins' departure, he was named Commander Military Assistance Command Vietnam (COMUS-MACV). His was a model career, but not necessarily one providing the proper experience for grasping political nuances. But then, given the system, who else was there?

However, President Johnson had not wholly accepted Westmoreland as Harkins' replacement. When Westy had gone to Saigon earlier as Harkins' deputy, he had not visited the White House. Some visitors such as Bernard Fall looked him over for the State Department and probably higher, to estimate whether he had the political skill to carry it off. Fall's report was favorable. Subsequently, in Honolulu, LBJ also appraised Westmoreland and concluded that he was not the type who would get involved in politics. "There's a lot riding on you," he told the General at that point. "I don't expect you to act like MacArthur."

Beginning in the late fall of 1964, events moved rapidly in Vietnam: two days before the United States election an enemy attack on the American base at Bien Hoa; and on Christmas an attack on the Brinks officers' hotel in downtown Saigon. By this time, with the election over, the President was considering his options. In late January McGeorge Bundy was dispatched to Saigon to look over the situation. Then came one of the benchmark events that seemed to set in motion a series of actions from which there was no turning back. On the afternoon (Washington time) of February 6, 1965, United States barracks and helicopters were subjected to surprise fire from the Viet Cong (the Pleiku incident), resulting in a substantial number of casualties. After receiving recommendations by phone from Taylor and Bundy in Saigon, LBJ decided to respond by aerial attack on North Vietnam. Senator Mike Mansfield had

8. *Swords and Plowshares*, p. 50

urged negotiation rather than military action, but the President was cool toward that idea.

In March, Marine ground units were dispatched to the Da Nang area as security for the Air Base, from which by now United States aircraft were conducting air missions in South as well as North Vietnam. Apparently, at this point there was no systematic consideration by Washington of the possibility of introducing ground troops. It is doubtful, however, that anyone with experience was unaware of the important threshold being crossed. Introduce combat organizations, and it is a long time indeed before they can be removed from a situation like that which existed in Vietnam at that time.

On April 17 President Johnson delivered a major policy address at Johns Hopkins University in which United States objectives in Southeast Asia were covered. It contained the statements:

> We are there because we have a promise to keep. Since 1954 every American president has offered support to the people of South Vietnam.

> Our objective is the independence of South Vietnam and its freedom from attack.

By late May reports from Vietnam began to take an ominous turn as word came in of ARVN units melting away in battle. By early June plans were under way to send 75,000 troops to Vietnam. By late June it was clear that Westmoreland felt the need for major reinforcements, and McNamara was dispatched to Vietnam to look at the situation. Events moved rapidly following his return. His report endorsed the view of going up to 150,000 troops by the end of 1965 and the possibility of exceeding 300,000 troops a year hence.

Shortly after McNamara's return, there was a meeting in the White House at which all officials involved expressed support of McNamara's recommendations. The climax came on July 28, 1965, when President Johnson addressed the nation concerning the troop reinforcement and redefined United States objectives in South Vietnam. He declared:

> We insist . . . that the people of South Vietnam shall have the right of choice, the right to shape their own destiny in free elections in the South, or throughout all Vietnam under inter-

national supervision, and they shall not have any government imposed upon them by force and terror so long as we can prevent it.

At this point LBJ introduced a new objective: "We intend to convince the Communists that we cannot be defeated by force of arms or by superior power." The President was laying United States prestige on the line.

By late summer the American troops were arriving. They included a corps-level headquarters, called a Field Force so as not to confuse it with a South Vietnamese Army Corps. The First Field Force was headed by soon-to-be Lieutenant General S. R. "Swede" Larsen, a West Pointer, class of 1939. Larsen also had had a spectacular career, going from a Captain in 1942 to a Colonel commanding a regiment in 1944. Not as well known as Westmoreland, he was still a comer in the fall of 1965. He was by nature impatient with mediocrity and lack of responsiveness—not necessarily traits that equipped him for dealing with ARVN. Nevertheless, he was highly regarded and did well in Vietnam, though as one of his associates said later, Vietnam was not a war Swede enjoyed.

Soon after General Larsen's arrival, he received his mission from Westmoreland in terms one might expect at the fighting level, but it is nevertheless revealing for its simplicity in such a complex environment: "Larsen, my guidance to you in the time you are here is you are to seek out the enemy and fight him wherever you can find him. I am not going to tell you specifics, but that should be your basic guidance to fight the war in II Corps."

Throughout 1966 and 1967 the basic objectives previously outlined remained pretty much the same while the United States troop build-up, eventually to exceed a half million, continued. To be sure, details were added which made the objectives more ambitious, and at the same time greater world support for the United States effort was sought. Nevertheless, when the Communist Tet Offensive came in early 1968, the formal objectives were still as set forth in NSAM 288 of March 1964.

The Tet offensive, as is well known, was the watershed of the Second Indo-Chinese War: a United States–GVN military victory in Vietnam, but a tremendous psychological defeat in the United States which brought down the Johnson Administration. The Johnson decision to restrict bombing in the North and to withdraw from the 1968 presidential election led the North Vietnamese to the conference table in Paris—and to a change in United States objectives (see below, pages 136–140). In brief, a limit to the United States commitment of forces was established, and the South Vietnamese were put on notice that in the future they would be expected to do more in their own defense.

For the first time, objectives were matched to the resources required to achieve the objectives, and the strategy was modified because the costs, both political and material, of attaining the objectives were considered excessive.

From the national policy objectives previously outlined, the JCS and COMUSMACV had derived the following military objectives by the time of the Tet Offensive:

(1) Deterring the Chinese from direct intervention in Southeast Asia.
(2) Defeating the Viet Cong and North Vietnamese Armed Forces in SVN and forcing the withdrawal of the NVA forces.
(3) Extending the Saigon government's control over all of South Vietnam.

It was clear after Tet 1968 that the United States could not destroy the enemy forces or force them completely from South Vietnam.

Not everyone drew this conclusion immediately. To some in the military, Tet seemed an opportunity to mobilize United States society and secure a military victory. By the civilian bureaucracy, however, Tet was read as a failure of policy which pointed up the need of the nation to get itself out of the Vietnam quagmire as soon as possible.

The survey that I undertook in 1974 directed two questions to the generals concerning objectives and received the following responses:

Were U.S. objectives in Vietnam prior to Vietnamization
(1969)   *Percentage*

(1) Clear and understandable	29
(2) Not as clear as they might have been	33
(3) Rather fuzzy—needed rethinking as the war progressed	35
(4) Other	3

Did lower echelons understand these objectives?

(1) Seemed to understand	20
(2) Understood imperfectly	57
(3) Not important—understanding important for them was day-to-day issues	20
(4) Other or no answer	3

Some typical commentary concerning those questions:

> We intervened with no clear idea of where we were headed. The Pentagon handling of the war was a play-it-by-ear gradual escalation.

> The national objective in Vietnam was never clear to anyone.

> Objectives lost meaning and were modified to justify events.

> The ultimate objective that emerged was the preservation of the U.S. leadership image and the maintenance of U.S. integrity in having committed itself; it could not then pull away from the quicksand in which it found itself.

> The U.S. was committed to a military solution, without a firm military objective—the policy was attrition—killing VC—this offered no solution—it was senseless.

Apparently, translating the overall United States objectives into something understandable to the general officers of the war was not successfully accomplished by policymakers. It is possible for lower-level soldiers and officials to fight a war without being sure of their objectives, but that almost 70 percent of the Army generals who managed the war were uncertain of its objectives mirrors a deep-seated strategic failure: the inability of policymakers to frame tangible, obtainable goals. It is relevant that, on a wrap-up question asking for proposed changes if the United States were to do it all over again, 91 percent called for a better definition of objectives.

One major objective of the leadership that conditioned all others was to keep the war limited, in the sense of not letting it escalate beyond Indo-China. Writing in 1966, Walter Lippmann stated that, given the course of United States actions in Vietnam, it was inevitable that the United States would find itself at war with China. This was a matter that had to be kept in mind, particularly in the earlier phases in the war, each time a decision involving escalation was being considered.

To a lesser extent, the Soviet Union also had to be considered. Generally it was felt that the Russians probably would not force a confrontation in Southeast Asia, since their vital interests were not clearly at stake. Of course, consideration always had to be given to the steps short of direct confrontation that the Soviet Union could take in response to United States escalation of the war. New and better weapons could have been provided to the North Vietnamese and the Viet Cong. There is no reason why the Soviets could not, for instance, have supplied the adversaries of the United States with small, shoulder-fired heat-seeking missiles (as they did after United States troops had left), thus increasing United States aircraft losses, especially helicopters. Alternatively, crises could have been instigated elsewhere—in Berlin or Korea, for instance. Obviously, the Kremlin leadership never felt it in their own self-interest to take such steps.

A further complication in deciding how far to go and still keep the war limited was the entire question of the interaction between the Soviet Union and China. Mining the North Vietnamese harbors had been suggested long before Nixon did so toward the end of the United States involvement. No doubt this would have given China additional influence over North Vietnam, since the remaining supply routes would have been through China. This influence would have been gained at the expense of the Soviet Union, which then would have been forced to decide what actions to take against the United States to reestablish its influence with Hanoi.

The foregoing considerations are mentioned because they conditioned both United States objectives and the manner in which they could be accomplished. Of more direct importance was how the war in the South was perceived in Hanoi and the strategy that the North Vietnamese and Viet Cong leadership employed to accomplish their own objectives.

The one overriding objective of the Hanoi leadership was the unification of Vietnam. After the French departure in 1954, this objective was bound to conflict with United States containment policy, which viewed the 17th parallel as a semipermanent cold-war boundary much like the 38th parallel in Korea. By mid-1955 Diem's anticommunist campaign was well under way and by late 1958 was making severe inroads on the Communists in the South. It was in this context that Hanoi decided that a political struggle alone was no longer enough. In January 1959 a decision was made in principle to resume armed revolt in the South primarily for Hanoi's own protection against the Diem regime.[9] By September 1960 increasing successes in the South caused Hanoi to move from the objective of protecting the Viet Cong to one of overthrowing Diem and establishing a coalition government. Within months the National Liberation Front was established in the South and the People's Liberation Army followed early in 1961. Increasing successes of the Viet Cong in 1961 brought about the Taylor-Rostow mission previously referred to.

Shortly after the overthrow of Diem in the fall of 1963, Hanoi called a meeting of the Central Committee, from which came important decisions with regard to the war in the South. Basically, it was decided to go on the offensive, and to provide increased assistance to the Viet Cong. The objective became a military victory, regardless of what the reaction of the United States might be. At the same time, the decision was made not to admit openly that North Vietnamese troops were or would be in the South.

The Hanoi analysis took into account the possibility of United States intervention with combat troops—an event that was still over a year off—but felt that such intervention would not change their objectives. Subsequently, in 1964, individual North Vietnamese soldiers were captured in Viet Cong units. By 1965 entire North Vietnamese regiments were detected in the Central Highlands, and by that fall they were in direct combat with United States forces.

What were Hanoi's stakes in the war and its specific objectives after the United States intervention? First, from an economic point of view, the economies of North and South Vietnam are complementary. Prior to the war the North did not have enough indigenous food sources to feed itself comfortably. The South was able to make up that deficit and still export rice abroad. The South, on the other hand, had no mineral resources and no industry, whereas the North had developed a small industrial base.[10]

From the North Vietnamese point of view, therefore, successful

9. This and subsequent decisions in 1960 and 1963 are excellently tied together in an article by King C. Chen, "Hanoi's Three Decisions and the Escalation of the Vietnam War," *Political Science Quarterly*, 90 (1975), 239–259.

10. P. H. M. Jones, "The Industry of North Vietnam," *Far Eastern Economic Review*, 29 (1960), 562 ff.

conclusion of the war would have a big payoff: a unified nation of more than 35 million, self-sufficiency in food, and a modest industrial base. Surely this prospect alone made the war a priority item in a way that it never could be to the American leadership. The war may have been a limited one from the United States point of view, but from the Hanoi perspective it was total.

By the time of the Tet offensive, therefore, the North Vietnamese objectives can be summarized as follows: First, to force the United States to stop bombing North Vietnam—not because the bombing would determine whether the North would win or lose, but because of its disruptive effects. More important was the desire to get United States forces out of Vietnam within a reasonable time. Another objective was to rebuild and extend the VC infrastructure in South Vietnam and, by so doing, to increase control over the rural population. Finally, there was the objective of weakening and discrediting the South Vietnamese government so as to reduce its effectiveness.

Since the war was viewed by Hanoi as political, all military operations were designed to support what eventually came to be negotiations with the Americans. In part, North Vietnamese policy included the standard techniques of coming to the conference table in the strongest possible position without making any real changes in objectives in order to do so. Additionally, it was based upon the United States political scene and the increasing fragmentation of American society as the war wore on.

In the survey there was a question designed to elicit views on whether United States officials took sufficient account of the enemy's determination to see the war through to his objectives:

Prior to 1968, the will and determination of the enemy to continue the war

	Percentage
(1) Was taken into account	20
(2) Was considered, but data were insufficient	19
(3) Was not sufficiently considered	56
(4) Other or no answer	5

Commentary on this question was fairly extensive:

A gross misconception by the United States of North Vietnamese capabilities, values, and determination.

Our political leaders did not properly assess the enemy's will.

Underestimated. We used "Western" standards—what would our people put up with?

His will was particularly bolstered by appearances of divisiveness and antiwar sentiment in the United States.

The enemy's will to continue varied directly in proportion to the dissidents and the uproar back home about continuing the war.

Criticism of the type voiced by Mansfield, Kennedy, Fulbright, et al., probably strengthened the enemy's resolve to do what he did subsequent to 1968.

I don't believe much effort was made to understand what the VC really meant to Vietnam.

Since we have viewed the conflicting objectives of the adversaries, it is appropriate to consider the controversial area of constraints which the United States placed on the application of its power. As we have said, certain of these constraints had to do with the desire to prevent the Soviet Union and China from becoming directly involved in the war. In part they also involved an attempt to secure United States objectives without destroying North Vietnam in the process, by inducing the enemy to come to terms and in the process to apply as little power as possible. The constraints may be grouped into three areas.

First, there are the rules of engagement themselves, to be discussed at greater length below (pages 51–55). These applied principally to operations within South Vietnam and came as a result of compromise between desirable military results and restrictive political and psychological factors. Such measures had as their immediate objectives avoidance of civilian casualties and property destruction by restricting the locations and conditions under which fire power could be applied in South Vietnam. Other restrictions existed on the use of chemical munitions and defoliants.

A second area of constraints covered cross-border operations into North Vietnam, Laos, and Cambodia. It was well known that the North Vietnamese line of communications went through neighboring countries and that Hanoi had established base areas contiguous to the South Vietnamese border. Nevertheless, for much of the war the United States did not operate with its ground troops in those areas—in effect, giving the enemy sanctuaries in which he could operate. As a result, in the period of 1965 to May 1970 the enemy had the great advantage of being able to fight the war his way. The reasons for this restraint have to do with attempts to avoid a bigger war and to accommodate public opinion at home and abroad.

A third area has to do with sea and air power. Until the final stage of negotiations, United States Presidents refrained from blockading North Vietnamese waters either by naval vessels or mining. There was less restriction on the application of air power, but there was some. For most of the war, there were restrictions on hitting certain targets in North Vietnam and there were repeated reversals, stopping and starting the bombing of the North.

That there has been considerable criticism of these constraints is well known. Typically, the critique runs something like this: "In the conduct of the war, let the tactical details of military operations be decided by military leaders without restriction, properly holding them responsible for the outcome."[11] One of the most trenchant criticisms of the constraints policy, of which the operational mode was gradualism, is Maxwell Taylor's:

> While this carefully controlled violence may have had some justification at the start, it ended by defeating its own purposes. Designed to limit the dangers of expanded war, it ended by assuring a prolonged war. . . . So gradualism encouraged the enemy to hang on until his hopes were fulfilled in 1968 by a collapse of the American will. . . . It may be that he knew Americans better than Americans knew themselves.
>
> If gradualism worked against the political purpose of inducing the enemy to seek an accommodation, it also violated the military principles of surprise and mass as a means to gain prompt support with minimum loss.[12]

Not all military commentators agree with the Taylor critique, but it seems to be salient among those who were responsible for fighting the war.[13] The Joint Chiefs, for example, conceived of all

11. Samuel P. Ingram, "Civilian Command or Civilian Control?" *United States Naval Institute Proceedings*, 94 (1968), 31.

12. *Swords and Plowshares*, pp. 403–404.

13. See, for example, Lt. Gen. Victor H. Krulak, "The Low Cost of Freedom," *United States Naval Institute Proceedings*, 96 (1970), 71, and General Hamilton H. Howze, "Vietnam: An Epilogue," *Army*, 25 (July 1975), 14.

kinds of actions which they believed would have accomplished
United States objectives in South Vietnam without widening the
war into a conflict with China or the USSR. In the main, they had
to do with more extensive air operations in North Vietnam and
Laos and naval operations against North Vietnam. In time many of
these actions came about, but not until 1970 in some cases and
1972 in others. The policy was a sore point with the military.

Commentary on this matter by survey respondents was in connection with another question on objectives:

Did you feel that United States objectives prior to
Vietnamization (1969) were: *Percentage*
  (1) Capable of achievement   43
  (2) Not capable of achievement   19
  (3) By 1968 not capable of achievement—should
     have been revised   25
  (4) Always should have been more limited   8
  (5) Other or no answer   5

Some commentary on this issue from the generals:

Impossible to fight with imposed constraints.

Too much civilian interference and restraints. We should
never have gone in under those circumstances.

Measured response was a total failure and surely a usurpation
of military ken by political incompetence.

The reason we failed was too much civilian interference in
military matters—too many constraints. We were in essence
handcuffed and not allowed to win.

If we had done all things initially, such as bombing Hanoi and
blockading Haiphong, as we did later incrementally, we
would have been more successful.

We should have been given far greater leeway in crossing
borders at least to raid. As you remember, McNamara denied
the correctness of my statement in May 1967 that there were
five to seven North Vietnamese regiments in Cambodia—a
deliberate and unnecessary lie to the American people.

Major error was to back into the war—a fear of Chinese involvement was at the heart of this. A clear intent to use our

then preemptive nuclear power would have been a strong counterbalance.

A final point that should be raised before concluding the discussion on objectives concerns the compatibility of United States and South Vietnamese objectives.[14] This is an important area to keep in mind when assessing later why events worked out the way they did. One thing is certain: the myth that the United States was calling the tune was just that. In reality there was a constant interaction between United States and GVN officials at all levels, with United States leverage probably becoming greater after Nixon's Vietnamization program began in 1969. That program presaged American disengagement and induced a greater sense of urgency in the Saigon regime.

As for South Vietnamese objectives during most of the period of intervention, they may be summarized as:

(1) Defeating the Communist attack.
(2) Maintaining and consolidating internal political control, especially over the rural population.
(3) Developing as much as possible the South Vietnamese economy.
(4) Securing as much foreign, especially United States, military and economic assistance as possible.

The foregoing goals must be viewed in a particular light. An overriding concern of the South Vietnamese leadership was their own survival and the consolidation of their power. For them this was not simply a war against Communism, as it may have been at times for the United States, but a war for survival. Viewed from this perspective, the goals require different priorities and sometimes different operational concepts than those held by the Americans.

In addition, the United States was never really able to penetrate the South Vietnamese decision-making processes. In part, this was a matter of GVN's view of its sovereign rights, but there were other reasons as well. The Vietnamese Joint General Staff, for

14. A good analysis of this question, upon which the following comments are based, is Lawrence E. Grintner's "Bargaining between Saigon and Washington: Dilemmas of Linkage Politics During War," *Orbis*, 18 (1974), 837–867. Grintner's analysis tends to confirm my own observations during my two years in Vietnam.

example, was able to resist successfully the notion of a joint United States–South Vietnamese Command. This permitted them largely to control their own assets, which on the materiel side were provided by the United States. In the area of economic assets, similar GVN controls prevailed.

Such leverage as the United States was able to bring to bear, was therefore, exerted chiefly through the advisory system, the strengths and weaknesses of which will be discussed in Chapter 4. This system was most effective during the period of Vietnamization, but it never penetrated the GVN decision-making processes, and its main effectiveness even then was in the technical aspects of the military effort.

The War in the South

Forces, Strategy and Tactics

At the end of 1964, with 23,000 United States troops in South Vietnam, President Johnson still had many options with respect to what course of action the United States should follow in order to stabilize the situation in that country. By midsummer of 1965 all the options were gone and only one course remained—to continue the United States build-up in South Vietnam. Eventually it was to reach 550,000 troops.

By New Year's Day 1965 it was evident to Westmoreland in Saigon that the United States concept of a limited commitment of Special Forces, helicopter, and other support to the indigenous forces was not going to be enough. Even before the Marine commitment in March, Westmoreland had made up his mind that he wanted combat troops. Early in the new year Brigadier General Ellis W. "Butch" Williamson, commander of the 173rd Airborne Brigade, stationed on Okinawa, flew to Saigon for some preliminary discussions. A unit was needed in the Bien Hoa area, Westmoreland felt, to secure the arrival and placement of other combat units if the President approved the commitment of combat forces.

A few weeks after the arrival of the Marines in early March, Ambassador Taylor was back in Washington for a meeting of the National Security Council on strategy in Vietnam. The bombing of the North, instituted by Lyndon Johnson in February, was obviously not having the desired effect on the North Vietnamese leadership, and the possibility of introducing United States ground troops was increasing. Taylor was opposed to a commitment of ground forces at that time, while the Joint Chiefs and Westmoreland were strong proponents of such a commitment.[1] Westmoreland himself was not in Washington for the meeting, but his able and persuasive J-3 operations chief, Brigadier William De Puy, was there to represent him before the Chiefs. The plan De Puy carried with him called for seventeen maneuver battalions to be sent to Vietnam as soon as possible.

The NSC meeting was held on April 1 and Taylor made a successful case against a troop commitment for the present. Westmoreland did get an additional two Marine battalions, together with some leeway as to how to employ the Marines, who heretofore had been restricted to base security missions. Such victory as Taylor achieved was short-lived. Events were now moving rapidly, and the military was pushing in concert for a troop build-up—Westmoreland from Saigon; Admiral U. S. Grant Sharp, technically Westmoreland's boss, from Honolulu, and the Joint Chiefs in Washington.

A key meeting which marked a watershed in the troop build-up occurred in Hawaii on April 20 with McNamara, Bundy from State, Chairman of the JCS Earle Wheeler, Sharp, Westmoreland, and Ambassador Taylor present. From the conference Westmoreland gained a commitment for 40,000 more troops, including the brigade he wanted for Bien Hoa, the 173rd Airborne. The floodgates were about to open. Meanwhile the situation continued to get worse for the ARVN—an ambush here, a defeat there, it seemed as though the South Vietnamese forces were coming unglued.

By June Westmoreland had requested forty-four maneuver battalions, which would increase the Honolulu commitment from a total authorized strength of about 80,000 to about 200,000. By late July, Johnson had made his decision—175,000 troops in Vietnam for the present. His announcement at a press conference on July 28 indicated only that the commitment would be increased to 125,000, and that others would be sent later.[2]

1. Taylor, a lifelong military professional, remained cautious on this point until the Honolulu conference of April 20, 1965. In large part his concern was what effect United States troops would have on South Vietnamese initiative and on the development of their military capabilities.

2. For Johnson's perspective on these early build-up decisions, see his *The Vantage Point*, (New York, Holt, Rinehart, and Winston, 1971), chap. 6.

Since Johnson's decisions were based on an assumption of no call-up of Reserves, the base from which to draw manpower for Vietnam was somewhat restricted. Westmoreland at one point had his staff in Saigon make their own estimate of the highest troop strength the United States could support in Vietnam without a mobilization. Their answer was a half million men. This, rather than any specific strategic or tactical plan, was the basis of the manpower goal which the Military Assistance Command sought.[3] Increase followed increase toward this goal through the years, each increase being called a program. The goal was called by Westmoreland "minimum essential forces," rather than the "optimum forces" of 670,000 which he occasionally requested but which was never seriously considered.

Each of these proposed increases had to be sold to Secretary McNamara, who early on told Westmoreland not to "worry about the economy of the country, the availability of forces, or public or Congressional attitudes." He, Westmoreland, should ask for what he felt was necessary to achieve his objectives, and McNamara would do his best to accommodate. After the decision was made and McNamara was back in Washington, he would pressure the Army to meet the request immediately. With no Reserves to call up, this threw the Army into a turmoil, in time wrecking the United States Army in Europe and the Army strategic reserve in the United States.

If the foregoing seems to indicate more preoccupation in Washington with how many troops were needed and the amount that could be provided rather than why they were needed, this is what the record shows. It is true that some officials outside the primary command circuit were concerned about what the ground troops were to do, but these individuals played no part in the real decision-making process. There was always some statement alluding to aims, put forward as justification for each troop-increase proposal, but the statements were so general as to be almost meaningless.

Approval of the deployment programs themselves, which are the benchmarks of decision-making in the war, related to size of forces alone; missions were not ruled on. Moreover, there is no

3. Of course, endless numbers of troop lists by type of unit could be and were produced to support one size of increase or another, but these were technical exercises and only in a gross sense were they related to strategic or tactical concepts or plans.

independent set of documents which deals with the question of precisely what the forces were for or how they were to be used. The original commitment of large-scale ground forces was an emergency measure, and subsequent increases were responses to a changing situation. Basically the increases were escalatory moves to compensate for enemy increases. The enemy in turn tried to compensate, and so it went, in what seemed for a time to be an endless cycle.

Not all external forces in South Vietnam were American. Washington perceived a need to show flags of friendly countries in South Vietnam, much as in Korea during the war there. Under pressure from the United States four Free World countries, as they were termed, contributed combat forces beginning in 1964, aggregating in 1969 a peak strength of 70,000 troops. Although small when compared with the United States contribution, this total was in fact larger than what other United Nations members contributed during the Korean War. The primary purpose of this program was political—to give the impression that it was not a United States war alone but involved other Asian nations in the cause of freedom. Except for the Australian–New Zealand contingent, which was self-supporting, this was an expensive operation for the United States.

The Korean forces, by far the largest of the Free World contingents—some 50,000 by 1969—were subsidized by the United States both directly and by enormous materiel outlays to modernize their forces back in Korea. The Koreans had a sector of their own along the coast in the II Corps Tactical Zone. They were professional, aggressive, and competent in combat. However, their insistence on overwhelming force superiority and long breaks between operations made them something less than cost-effective. They also were a problem. Their image among the South Vietnamese was not always good and, as I will discuss subsequently, their adherence to the rules of engagement was, allegedly, not always precise. However, within this framework they did their job well.

The Australian Task Force was competent, particularly in training ARVN units. One of their early commanders foolishly planted thousands of mines around their area in Phuoc Tuy Province in the III Corps Tactical Zone (the eleven provinces around Saigon). At a small cost in life, the VC learned how to defuse these mines and eventually employed them defensively against the Task Force with a fair degree of success. As time went on and the war became more unpopular with the Australian public, the effectiveness of this force decreased. Commanders were reluctant to employ their troops in real operations where casualties might occur. As a result, the force took to what was known as "swanning around," a large-scale equivalent of what used to be called "soldiering" in an early period of the American labor movement.

The least effective Free World combat force was the division from Thailand.[4] Like the Korean forces, this unit was heavily subsidized by the United States. The division operated in Bien Hoa province in the vicinity of Bear Cat. They posed black market problems of various sorts and, unlike the Koreans, could not or would not fight. As one senior American commander said in a moment of frustration, "They are protecting the VC. If I could get them out of there for a while, I could clean out the Cong in that area."

Lest the reader gain the wrong impression from the frank nature of the foregoing comments, it should be said that these Free World forces were on balance probably worth having in Vietnam, certainly from a political view. Even from a technical military view, they were probably worthwhile. Many individuals and units fought well. The Koreans and Aussies had good control of their areas, especially the Koreans. From the Thais perhaps we expected too much.

In the summer of 1967 LBJ, feeling the need for additional Free World support, dispatched Clark Clifford and Maxwell Taylor on a Pacific tour. The allies were not much interested in their message.[5] As Clifford says, "It was strikingly apparent to me that the other troop-contributing countries no longer shared our degree of concern about the war in South Vietnam. General Taylor and I urged them to increase their participation. In the main our plea fell on deaf ears."[6]

The announced rationale for the initial deployments of United States ground units was for the security of United States bases and

4. More precisely divisions, since there was rotation of units back to Thailand and their replacement by fresh units.

5. Subsequently Korea and Australia made slight increases and Thailand a substantial increase, but this latter increment probably included forces already programmed.

6. Clark M. Clifford, "A Viet Nam Reappraisal," *Foreign Affairs* 47 (1969), 606.

installations in South Vietnam. These were bases whose aircraft were primarily involved in Rolling Thunder, the bombing of North Vietnam. By the time most of the deployments were under way, however, the rationale had shifted. In the first place, Rolling Thunder, as previously mentioned, was not meeting the expectations of its proponents in bringing Hanoi to negotiations. Further, there was at the same time a deteriorating military situation in South Vietnam.

During the NSC meetings on April 1 and 2, 1965, the President had approved Westmoreland's use of ground force units as far out as fifty miles from the bases in order to support South Vietnamese forces and keep the enemy off balance. Shortly afterward the President also approved Westmoreland's search-and-destroy strategy, a concept that in time was to become controversial but which was based on principles which the United States had employed routinely in other more conventional wars. The basic idea was to take the war to the enemy and by using superior United States mobility and firepower to seize the initiative and inflict heavy losses on enemy units. Behind this screen the South Vietnamese forces would operate in the more populated areas. The latter point was an important change of concept (eventually to have profound results) as the strategy shifted during the summer of 1965. The security or enclave strategy, as some prefer to call it, had been designed to deny the enemy victory. Search and destroy soon had as its goal defeat of the enemy in the South by United States forces.

Westmoreland himself was later to deny that search and destroy was even a strategy. It was, he told Townsend Hoopes, only one of three basic types of operations, the other two being clearing and securing operations. The objective of clearing operations was to drive large enemy units out of populated areas so that pacification could proceed. Such operations normally did not completely clear areas of local guerrilla units; securing operations were required to protect pacification teams and to eliminate local guerrilla units. Although the clearing operations were normally conducted by regular South Vietnamese forces, the securing operations were usually conducted by Regional and Popular Forces or the police.

In this context, then, Westmoreland's idea was to conduct search-and-destroy operations at some distance from the populated areas. These were aimed at the enemy forces and their base and at supply areas in the jungle and mountains. They were designed to keep the enemy off balance, as well as to preempt his attack plans and prevent him from returning to the populated areas.

One of the problems with the search-and-destroy strategy was the open-ended nature of the commitment. If the objective is to defeat an enemy force rather than denying it victory, then the eventual cost depends as much on the enemy as on one's own plans. It in effect depends upon what price the enemy—in this case, North Vietnam—is willing to pay. The more he is willing to pay in terms of manpower, the more one must increase one's own units.

I have earlier made reference to the general support of the Joint Chiefs for the Westmoreland position. Search and destroy in Vietnam was, however, an Army concept. It meant in effect that the United States Army would bear the brunt of fighting the war in South Vietnam, with the Republic of Vietnam forces stepping aside, at least until the North Vietnamese–Viet Cong had been dealt a major blow. Although JCS records are not available, it is generally known that the Air Force Chief of Staff and the Marine Commandant were in favor of the security or enclave strategy, whereas the Army Chief and the Chairman, Army General Earle Wheeler, favored search and destroy.[7]

One of the principal architects of United States tactics and strategy in the Vietnamese War was Brigadier General De Puy. A non-West Pointer with a bachelor's degree from South Dakota State College, class of 1941, De Puy became a regular officer at the end of World War II, having served in Europe as an Infantry Officer during the war. For a number of years he worked in the intelligence field, including a stint with the CIA in Washington.

In the late 1950's he served in the Chief of Staff's Office, as did Westmoreland, and made a very favorable impression on the future COMUSMACV. Later, when Westmoreland needed an officer to be his J-3 in Saigon, he requested De Puy, who in the interim had attended the British Imperial Defense College and had been promoted to Brigadier General.

An intense person of boundless energy and great ambition, De Puy was inclined to paint with a rather broad brush. As a staff officer, he always did his homework and was both articulate and convincing. Westmoreland considered him brilliant. De Puy was convinced in the early days of United States troop involvement in Vietnam that the answer to success was the massive deployment of

7. *PP*, Vol. 3, p. 397.

United States troops. If Westmoreland needed any convincing, De Puy was there to provide it. Inclined toward introspection, he told me after the war had ended that he had not been perspicacious enough in those days. We should, he said, have thought through the military problem better.

Through 1965 and well into 1966 the continuing build-up of North Vietnamese forces was Westmoreland's major preoccupation. There seems little doubt that without the United States intervention, the South Vietnamese would not have made it past 1965. It was in this context that Westmoreland committed the newly arrived 1st Cavalry Division (Airmobile) to the Central Highlands in September 1965. The First Team, as it was known, engaged in the first major United States battle in the war. Although the provinces in the highlands are sparsely populated, they are important, as we saw in the spring of 1975. They serve in effect as a gateway to the Saigon area, and it is only a short distance across the narrow waist of the country to the important coastal provinces.

Westmoreland committed the Air Cavalry division on the basis of intelligence that three North Vietnamese divisions coming out of Cambodia were going to link up with the VC in the coastal province of Binh Dinh. In what became known as the battle of Ia Drang Valley, the Air Cavalry reportedly killed almost 2,000 Vietnamese military and forced the remainder back into their sanctuaries in Cambodia.

Thereafter, in 1965 and 1966, as the troop build-up continued, the overall military situation began to stabilize to some extent. During the last half of 1966 and all of 1967 United States troop strength went from just under 400,000 to just under 500,000 and was employed with two general objectives in mind. The first was the destruction of enemy bases, particularly those surrounding Saigon, such as War Zone C, the Iron Triangle,[8] and War Zone D. The Viet Cong had long enjoyed immunity in those areas, living underground and able to emerge from their bases to terrorize the population, recruit replacements, or harass government forces. These havens, Westmoreland decided, had to be neutralized. The other effort of the big war period was against major North

8. The Iron Triangle, smaller than either War Zone C or D, was pointed toward Saigon. It was bounded on two sides by rivers and on the third by jungle. It was completely tangled with vines and a complex of underground tunnels, rooms, hospitals, printing presses, and fighting positions. Thousands of VC could occupy it.

Vietnamese units as they emerged from time to time from sanctuaries in Cambodia, Laos, and the Demilitarized Zone.

The first large-scale operation occurred by accident in War Zone C east of Tay Ninh City in November 1966. It involved some 22,000 United States troops and was directed against the Viet Cong 9th Division. Over 3,000 Viet Cong were reported killed, wounded, or captured, and the division was put out of action for six months. Although only by chance did the operation develop to the scale it did, the lesson drawn was that large-scale operations clearly had a place in counterinsurgency warfare. Thereafter two such operations, controlled by II Field Force Vietnam (the United States Tactical Command operating in the Vietnamese Third Corps Tactical Zone surrounding Saigon), were planned and executed in succession: Cedar Falls against the Iron Triangle base area north and west of Saigon in January 1967, and Junction City in War Zone C north of Tay Ninh City from February to May 1967. These preplanned operations involved large numbers of United States troops and the use of massive firepower.[9]

In a technical sense, the operations were highly successful, but nothing could prevent the enemy from later returning to the areas, since the United States of necessity had to evacuate the bases when the action was over. It would have taken a United States force of one million to permanently occupy ground previously fought over. It is for operations of this type, as contrasted with emergency actions such as the Ia Drang Valley battle, that Westmoreland has been criticized, justly or unjustly. To this criticism I now wish to turn.

Westmoreland's strategy in Vietnam has been subject to extensive commentary from a wide variety of sources. Before hearing what his own generals had to say about certain aspects of his strategy, it will be useful to view a sample of the external critique. In the main, commentary has focused on the inadvisability of a strategy of attrition. Other facets have been singled out for criticism, however, such as suffering high casualties in seizing a piece

9. One volume of the Vietnam Study series put out by the United States Army concerns these engagements: Lt. Gen. Bernard W. Rogers, *Cedar Falls—Junction City: A Turning Point* (Washington, Government Printing Office, 1974). Note the irony of the subtitle. Cedar Falls is described from a different perspective in less glowing terms by Jonathan Schell, *The Village of Ben Suc* (New York, Knopf, 1967).

of terrain only to evacuate it thereafter, and in another vein the overdependence of United States forces on technology.

Henry Kissinger was one of the better known critics of attrition, writing in *Foreign Affairs*: "American military strategy followed the classic doctrine that victory depended on a combination of control of territory and attrition of the opponent . . . The theory was that the defeat of the main forces would cause the guerrillas to wither on the vine. Victory would depend on inflicting casualties substantially greater than those we suffered until Hanoi's losses became 'unacceptable'." He went on to develop the thought that the attrition strategy (the success of which after all depended on the will and determination of the enemy) brought military successes that could not be translated into political advantage.[10] For his part, Westmoreland never felt that Kissinger understood that operations aimed at attriting the enemy's main force units went hand in hand with actions aimed at the guerrilla infrastructure, and so advised Lyndon Johnson at one point. Sir Robert Thompson, another critic of the American strategy, points out that though the search-and-destroy strategy achieved commendable results on the casualty graphs, it permitted Hanoi to hold the strategic initiative by accepting the casualties in order to achieve her political aim.[11]

A more pungent criticism appeared in, of all places, a West Point text written by a lieutenant colonel instructor: "But one thing should be made absolutely clear: attrition is not a strategy. It is irrefutable proof of the absence of any strategy. A commander who resorts to attrition admits his failure to conceive of an alternative. He turns from warfare as an art and accepts it on the most nonprofessional terms imaginable. He uses blood in lieu of brains. Saying that political considerations forced the employment of attrition warfare does not alter the hard truth that the United States was strategically bankrupt in Vietnam."[12]

Westmoreland's strategy was also attacked from another angle. Since not all of Vietnam could be occupied by troops, terrain fea-

10. Henry Kissinger, "The Viet Nam Negotiations," *Foreign Affairs* 47 (1969), 212.

11. Thompson, *No Exit from Vietnam*, p. 135.

12. Lt. Colonel Dave Richard Palmer, *Readings in Current Military History* (West Point, Department of Military Art and Engineering, 1969), p. 94. Many other critics thinking along these lines could be cited, such as Townsend Hoopes, formerly Under Secretary of the Air Force, and Brian Jenkins of The RAND Corporation.

tures containing troops were frequently attacked and then relinquished after the enemy was defeated. Senator Kennedy referred to such an approach as "senseless and irresponsible." One of the more publicized attacks of this nature was in the A Shau Valley against Ap Bia, which the airborne troops named "Hamburger Hill."[13] Critics recognized the doctrinal soundness of the operation, which was designed to clear the enemy from the A Shau valley in general and Ap Bia in particular, in order to eliminate a base that could be used for further assaults on Hue and Da Nang. They point out, however, that its cost in lives and the disastrous public image of the American effort created in consequence make it an outstanding example of a misplaced strategy. Such an operation, they suggest, might have been accomplished, perhaps less conclusively, by firepower alone; in any case, its execution lacked stealth and tactical finese.

Still another area of criticism of Westmoreland's strategy has to do with the Americanization of the war, which will be discussed in a later chapter. A few words are in order here. Most agree that when Westmoreland committed the Air Cavalry division in the Ia Drang Valley in September 1965, the situation was tenuous indeed. Sometime in 1966, however, the military situation had stabilized to the point where the South Vietnamese forces could have been increasingly committed but were not. The United States forces simply pushed the South Vietnamese out of the war and took over the combat effort. In part this Americanization of the war was encouraged by the many technological innovations introduced by United States forces. These innovations included various types of aircraft, naval vessels, and detection devices which at that point only United States personnel could operate and in the long run only United States personnel could maintain.[14] In effect, then, the allegation is that we invented a form of war which only we could fight and which was irrelevant to long-term political objectives. Later, when our forces had to leave Vietnam, our heritage to our ally was a form of warfare he could not sustain.

Sixty-two percent of the Army general officers who responded to the questionnaire thought that the tactics employed could have

13. This particular attack occurred after Westmoreland had departed from Vietnam, but it was similar to others that had taken place earlier.

14. For some unusually perceptive comments on this issue, see R. W. Komer, *Bureaucracy Does Its Thing* (Santa Monica, RAND, 1972), chap. 7.

been improved in a major way. In addition, three specific questions pertaining to tactics were included.

Was the search and destroy concept	*Percentage*
(1) Sound	38
(2) Sound when first implemented—not later	26
(3) Not sound	32
(4) Other or no answer	4

Execution of search and destroy tactics was	
(1) Superior	7
(2) Adequate	35
(3) Left something to be desired	51
(4) Other or no answer	7

How do you feel about the large-scale operations (Attleboro, Cedar Falls, etc.)?	
(1) Use early in war correct	28
(2) Should have been continued	21
(3) Overdone from the beginning	42
(4) Other or no answer	9

These replies show a noticeable lack of enthusiasm, to put it mildly, by Westmoreland's generals for his tactics and by implication for his strategy in the war. Most of the commentary was concerned with the third question.

Largely ineffective due to enemy intelligence activities.

Large-scale operations were correct but should have been employed against specific objectives in North Vietnam and not against a will o' the wisp enemy in some unstrategic jungle.

Depending upon enemy situation and availability of troops, these operations served an important purpose, such as along the border of Laos in the north in 1969–70. Here again, however, the press created a false impression.

One four-star general commented on this matter as follows:

The basic errors were made in 1965–66 when United States troops were committed piecemeal all over South Vietnam with no clear-cut tactical mission. Even in 1967 it was not too late to change the basic strategy, i.e. employ most United States forces in the north (including Laos) to insulate South Vietnam from the North. At the same time put a massive effort into upgrading the South Vietnamese forces for their task of wearing down the VC—who would no longer be constantly reinforced, reindoctrinated, retrained, and resupplied from the North.

Implements of War

Another loudly voiced criticism of the war in South Vietnam has concerned the implements of warfare: firepower, especially the quantity employed; herbicides; and CS gas (a type of tear gas). The substitution of firepower for maneuver in order to minimize casualties in Vietnam was to some extent understandable. A conscript army in an unpopular war must minimize casualties if it is going to sustain even marginal public support. Even apart from the loss of tactical initiative which this substitution brings, however, if it is carried too far, there are many undesirable side effects.

When one considers that the total munitions employed by the United States in Vietnam was greater than tonnages employed worldwide in the 1941–45 war, some of these side effects on a populated country the size of Vietnam are not difficult to imagine. Technically, the firepower was used effectively on a high percentage of occasions; but the use of air and artillery, even though many controls were imposed, could not but alienate a good portion of the civilian population whom we were trying to win over. There is no question that the firepower was to some extent politically counterproductive; the problem is at what point was it overdone? Another side effect was the bad habit acquired by the South Vietnamese forces: they learned the expensive habit of employing vast amounts of munitions—a habit that in the final years could not be sustained as U.S. support was gradually reduced.

One of the more expensive and least effective techniques of employing artillery fire was what was known as harassing and interdiction (H and I) fires. These were fires routinely used at night on targets selected with the end in mind of assisting in the defense of friendly installations. They became a particular target of criticism

for Edward Kennedy, not so much because of their cost but because at times they were near populated areas. There were, of
course, restrictions on firing into the populated areas themselves.

After a trip to Vietnam, Kennedy saw Lyndon Johnson in
January 1968 and raised the question of interdiction fires in a
broader context. There were, he told the President, differences in
views among the general officers in Vietnam about the tactics being
employed. As an illustration, he brought up the H and I fires,
which he felt were being overdone. Thereafter, these types of fires
were curtailed somewhat, but not entirely. They were renamed
"intelligence targets" to give the impression that they were based
on much better information of the enemy than the previous H and
I fires. That they were is questionable, [15] but at least the quantity of
ammunition expended on this type of target was reduced.

One question was included in the survey concerning views on
close air support, and one on artillery support.

Was close air support	*Percentage*
(1) About right quantitatively	64
(2) Not enough quantitatively	6
(3) Too much considering the nature of the war	28
(4) Other or no answer	2

Was artillery support	
(1) About right	57
(2) Not enough	10
(3) Too much considering the nature of the war	30
(4) Other or no answer	3

What is surprising in these figures is that a substantial minority
of the generals themselves felt that there was too much firepower.
Commentary was in the main directed toward the artillery question. In particular, comments were very critical of H and I fires;
one respondent said such fires were "madness."

15. In May 1969 I returned to Vietnam as Commanding General of II
Field Force Artillery. On my second day in the country I asked to have
the intelligence targets plotted on my map. Afterward, I asked to see the
person who selected the targets, together with the data on which he based
his selections. A 1st Lieutenant appeared with a coordinate square; in-
specting a map, he selected, at random, points in the areas where night-
time firing was authorized, and then measured off the coordinates for
firing. This had been the method of choosing intelligence targets in that
zone for the preceding several months.

One element of firepower that was in a category of its own was the B-52. Part of the United States strategic triad, along with the Polaris Fleet Ballistic Missile System and Intercontinental Ballistic Missiles, this aircraft was employed extensively during the Vietnam War in its conventional mode. In the spring of 1965 General Westmoreland, with Ambassador Taylor's political endorsement, made his case for the employment of the big bombers in South Vietnam. The case was based on the need for effective pattern bombing of VC installations in jungle areas, which could best be carried out by the B-52 weapons system. Despite some misgivings on the part of the SAC Commander and the Air Force Staff, who did not want to see the strategic deterrent deteriorate, Westmoreland's proposal was approved in Washington, The first bombing raid was conducted in June 1965 against War Zone D. Thereafter the ARC LIGHT program, as the B-52 bombing was called, became a regular part of the war.[16]

Demand for ARC LIGHT strikes always exceeded availability (which could go as high as sixty planes per day) and allocation to the competing claimants was closely controlled by Westmoreland's headquarters. Target selection was based on the overall enemy situation as well as on the importance of the target and the reliability of the intelligence sources by which the target was located. It was a relatively blunt instrument and, as in all bombing of jungles, there was frequently no way of knowing the precise nature of the target—hospital, strategic area, or troop-training area.

In judging the effectiveness of the program, the survey respondents seemed in general favorably inclined, although clearly many did not think the program vital.

B-52 strikes in South Vietnam were	Percentage
(1) Very valuable	47
(2) Useful but not vital	36
(3) Not worth the effort	15
(4) Other or no answer	2

Comments covered a wide spectrum from "the most decisive single element" to "not worth the effort when considered in the light of what it did to the people and territory of South Vietnam." Judgment of this issue perhaps more than of most depended on the location from which one viewed the program. This is illustrated by the comments of one of the generals.

16. *PP*, Vol. 3, pp. 383, 384.

In my first tour B-52s were nor particularly decisive. They added to our arsenal of weapons significantly but I can't see where they spelled the difference between success and failure in any operation. During my second tour they were decisive and enabled us to stop the advance of the NVA toward Hue and to retake Quang Tri in 1972.

Defoliation through the use of herbicides was extensively employed in Vietnam to deny the enemy concealment, hence to increase the effectiveness of United States firepower. Herbicides were originally used against jungle areas to expose the camps and infiltration routes and along the sides of waterways and highways. Subsequently, the program was expanded to destroy enemy crops so as to divert his combat efforts to food procurement and supply. Land clearing by herbicides was supplemented by the use of large plows, called Rome Plows (developed in Rome, Georgia).

Although employment of the plows received some criticism because of their permanent ecological impact, most of the discussion in the press and in journals was concerned with herbicides, which were used much more excessively than the plows. Arguments against their use were set forth at two levels: their ecological impact, and the allegation that their use violated international law.

The first argument pointed out the permanent susceptibility to herbicides of mangrove and to a lesser extent other types of forests, and the subsequent bamboo invasion of areas experiencing a high tree loss, which in turn could retard or prevent an area from returning to its natural state. In time the United States heeded the warnings of the environmentalists and by 1969 had almost phased out the herbicide-spraying program. In any event, use from that time on was tightly controlled both as to type of agent and to the extent of its use.

The other argument concerned the legal status of herbicides, as well as of CS gas, a lachrymatory or tear gas used to incapacitate the enemy in such situations as flushing out a tunnel. Both herbicides and CS gas were, its opponents alleged, violations of the Geneva Protocol of 1925. This was a protocol forbidding the use of gas warfare to which the United States did not adhere until 1975. To accuse the United States, not then technically bound by the Protocol, of violating the norms of international law, one must make a broad interpretation of the applicability of international law. There is also the further problem of whether herbicides or CS came within the intent of the Protocol. On both issues the experts were and are in disagreement.[17] In any case, the CS gas was used throughout the war, and although the public relations aspects were watched carefully, it was generally felt by respondents to the questionnaire that the CS issue was blown out of proportion. A substantial minority did accept the argument that if elimination of CS would help in acceptance of the Geneva Protocol by the United States, it was a marginal enough program to be given up for important political reasons.

In commenting on the questions concerning CS and land clearing, the generals were terse and pragmatic. "Why worry about tear gas," one commented, "when we were shooting bullets?" There was some negative commentary on the extent of the herbicide clearing, but it was not frequently voiced. The responses show a substantial minority against herbicides, with more approval shown for Rome plows and CS gas.

Were herbicides as used in Vietnam *Percentage*
  (1) Necessary when used, and controls imposed
     were about correct   53
  (2) More controls should have been imposed   20
  (3) Not worth their value considering physical damage
     they caused   21
  (4) Other or no answer   6

Use of Rome Plows was
  (1) About right, and they were properly controlled   43
  (2) There should have been more Rome plow companies   37
  (3) A questionable program except in some select
     areas, considering physical side effects   16
  (4) Other or no answer   4

Was CS gas
  (1) A necessary assist for small units which should not
     have been given up for any reason   63
  (2) Could have been given up for larger political objectives such as overall restrictions on chemical warfare   29
  (3) Other or no answer   8

17. These and related issues are explored at some length in Peter D. Trooboff, ed., *Law and Responsibility in Warfare* (Chapel Hill, N.C., University of North Carolina Press, 1975).

There was one implement of warfare not used—atomic weapons. Some comment seems in order. National Security Council papers in 1953 and 1954 discuss in general terms the employment of nuclear weapons as a possibility in hypothetical situations, such as the Chinese Communists overrunning Indochina.[18] There was also some general discussion of the possibility in various meetings of high-level officials before the American troop intervention.[19] I am unable to find any evidence, however, that their employment was ever seriously considered in Washington. From Westmoreland's memoirs it is evident that there was some study at one point on their possible use in the Khe Sanh battle. As he indicated, when Washington received word of this possibility, he was told to desist.[20]

Rules of Engagement

Fighting a war on the scale we have described, while utilizing an intensive munitions approach, was bound to be disruptive to South Vietnamese society and to inflict heavy casualties upon it. The nature of the war and the desire both to keep the conflict limited and to hold civilian casualties to a minimum prompted American forces to adopt self-imposed restrictions. These were known as "rules of engagement." Although the South Vietnamese forces were not specifically bound by them, efforts were made at every level by American advisers to obtain compliance with these rules.

Some of the rules were imposed by the Joint Chiefs of Staff, primarily those designed to keep the war limited and to avoid international incidents. JCS-imposed rules, for example, dealt with operations in border areas and within the Demilitarized Zone. The JCS also prescribed specifications for strikes by B-52 bombers in South Vietnam, including the restrictions that a target must be at least one kilometer from any locality inhabited by noncombatants.

Westmoreland published more than forty directives of his own which contained explicit guidance on proper treatment of civilians and their property as well as on a discriminating use of firepower. The fighting environment, which provided no line of contact with

18. *PP*, Vol. 1, pp. 88, 466, 512.
19. *PP*, Vol. 2, pp. 322; Vol. 3, pp. 175, 238.
20. Westmoreland, *A Soldier Reports*, p. 338.

the enemy, had not been encountered by United States forces since before World War I. What was required was a fairly elaborate system of checks and clearances with local officials prior to subjecting an area to intensive firepower. There were also other areas, usually fairly remote, which after clearance was once obtained from South Vietnamese officials were routinely subjected to fire without additional political clearance. These were known as "free fire zones" or "specified strike zones."

There was no shortage of directives on this subject from 1965 onward. Westmoreland himself stressed the matter before his commanders on many occasions, the most notable being a commanders' conference held in late August 1966. "It is extremely important that we do all we can to use our fires with discrimination, and avoid noncombatant battle casualties. This is a very sensitive subject, both locally and among our own press corps," he said.

Notwithstanding these directions and admonitions, many allegations have been made that the United States Army in Vietnam countenanced numerous violations of its own rules. One criticism holds that whatever official policy may have been, many war crimes (as distinct from unintentional violations) were committed and went unpunished; therefore the implicit policy was other than officially stated.[21] Herbert Kelman writes: "The My Lai massacre, however, was not an isolated, aberrant event. Similar actions were not uncommon in Vietnam, in fact they were an inevitable by-product of the very nature of the war."[22] A retired Army officer wrote in the same vein: "My Lai represented to the average professional soldier nothing more than being caught in a cover-up of something which he knew had been going on for a long time on a smaller scale."[23]

A more specific indictment of the chain of command in Vietnam appeared in an article in the *New York Times* on November 29, 1971, in connection with the court martial trial of Colonel Oran K. Henderson, one of the My Lai defendants. The author of the article, Douglas Robinson, contended that both the defense and prosecution carefully avoided discussion of probable deficiency in the command structure in Vietnam. While there was "command em-

21. "Who's Really Guilty in My Lai Case: G. I. Defendants or Military System?" *Philadelphia Inquirer*, November 15, 1970.

22. Herbert C. Kelman, "The Military Establishment," *Society* (May/June 1975), pp. 18–22.

23. King, *The Death of the Army*, p. 122.

phasis" on avoiding war crimes, Robinson said, neither MACV nor its subordinate headquarters had a system set up to ensure compliance with Westmoreland's rules of engagement directives.

Whether it represented an aberration or not, My Lai was the most publicized atrocity in the Vietnam War, and without doubt by far the largest. The story has been widely told, and I will recount only certain aspects as background before considering the generals' responses to questions on rules of engagement.

During the period March 16-19, 1968, a tactical operation was conducted into Son My Village, Son Tinh District, Quang Ngai Province, by Task Force Barker, a battalion-size unit of the Americal Division. The plans for the operation were never reduced to writing, but it seems to have been aimed at destroying a VC local force battalion thought to be located in Son My Village.

The operation, which later became notorious, took place on the morning of March 16 and resulted in the massacre of a large number of Vietnamese nationals (but not the local force battalion) in the village of Son My. Though the picture is not clear who subsequently was informed of the atrocity, what seems clear is that within the Americal Division efforts were made to conceal from higher authority what happened that morning in Son My.

There the matter rested until late March 1969 when Ron Ridenhour wrote to the Secretary of Defense and others setting forth allegations concerning the massacre of the year before. Eventually an investigative group was established by the Army to look into the massacre and the cover-up that followed. Lieutenant General William R. Peers was selected to head the group. An excellent choice for the task, Peers had commanded both the 4th Division in Vietnam and I Field Force during the period 1967–69. A graduate of UCLA in 1937, Peers had the appearance, mannerisms, and instincts of a frontiersman. A good football player in college, he made up for his lack of size with courage. He had proven to be "a dynamic commander" in Vietnam, to use Westmoreland's words. A straightforward and pragmatic individual, he worked well with the Vietnamese.

In any case, his final report on the massacre, submitted in March 1970, is a masterpiece of lucidity and scathing in regard to the cover-up within the Americal Division. The outcome is well known; it involved only one guilty court-martial verdict, that of Lieutenant William Calley. Several high-ranking officers were reprimanded, in effect terminating their careers. General Samuel Koster, the division commander, lost a star and subsequently retired as a Brigadier General.

One of the forces in Vietnam that had a particular reputation for brutality, although facts are hard to come by, was the South Koreans. Information was difficult to obtain, since their areas of operation were not opened to unescorted observers with the same freedom as were the United States and South Vietnamese areas of operation. Although the United States headquarters was not responsible for the day-to-day operations of the Koreans, nevertheless the United States Government did bear a certain responsibility for its role in bringing this force to Vietnam and subsidizing its operations. There was a flurry of stories concerning Korean brutality and atrocities in the newspapers in early 1970; they were revived again about two years later. There seems little doubt that Korean brutalities and killings occurred approximately as alleged in these articles. American observers recount discussions with South Vietnamese civilians and military who expressed anger and bitterness at the conduct of the Koreans. There are anecdotes by the dozen, but they are hearsay, since, as I have noted, foreigners were not allowed to wander around the Korean area of operations.

In September 1974 when the generals answered the questionnaire, My Lai and other war crimes allegations were no longer in the news. Considering the nature of the subject, a surprisingly large number of respondents answered these questions. Additional commentary was, however, notable for its absence. What stands out in the responses is that despite many directives, or perhaps because of them, the rules were not very well understood, nor were they carefully adhered to.

Before My Lai the rules of engagement were   *Percentage*
  (1) Well understood throughout the chain of command   29
  (2) Fairly well understood throughout the chain of command   49
  (3) Frequently misunderstood throughout the chain of command   17
  (4) Other or no answer   5

Before My Lai became public knowledge, the rules of engagement were
  (1) Carefully adhered to throughout the chain of command   19

Command and Control

One of the more unusual aspects of the war in Vietnam was the arrangements for commanding and controlling the forces from Washington right on down to the fighting units themselves. As Komer has pointed out, by and large Washington managed the war in Vietnam pretty much with a peacetime structure,[24] with emphasis on ad hoc rather than systematic arrangements. When Ambassador Taylor returned to Washington from Saigon, he attempted to strengthen the State Department's role in managing the war. As he points out, he was unsuccessful in implementing this aim, notwithstanding approval by the President of a document that set up an interdepartmental committee designed in part to improve management of the war at the Washington level.[25] After the Nixon Administration took office, there was increased centralization both in Kissinger's White House staff and in the Department of Defense. These efforts led to more systematic Washington-level management, but they were mainly concerned with the United States disengagement rather than providing guidance in fighting the war.

There is some evidence that the American Commander in Vietnam was not particuarly interested in getting more detailed or systematic guidance from Washington. In September 1965 he reacted unfavorably to a message from the State Department which raised some questions about how the counterinsurgency campaign was being conducted. Westmoreland viewed these questions as perhaps "violating" his "prerogatives as commander." The Washington message, he felt, was another example of people coming up with ideas who were "dealing from an ivory tower environ-

24. Komer, pp. 79 ff.
25. Taylor, *Swords and Plowshares*, pp. 360–363.

ment." Westmoreland regretted such tendencies and did all he could to discourage them.

On the other hand, Westmoreland was satisfied with the Joint Chiefs, and especially of General Wheeler, in their role as the supervising agency of the war in Vietnam. One of the Joint Chiefs during this period told me that he had felt like an "observer" and, despite a sense of responsibility for what was happening, had little feeling of control over the war itself.

Between Washington and Westmoreland's headquarters in Saigon there was an intermediate official in Hawaii, Commander-in-Chief Pacific (CINPAC). Sometimes Westmoreland's headquarters dealt directly with Washington but usually he had to deal through CINPAC. There was a peculiar aspect in the conduct of the war by which the commander in Hawaii was responsible for the air war in the North. In effect, there were two military commanders fighting two different wars. Westmoreland considered that the split between the two wars was unsound, but there were, he felt, enough practical reasons to keep him from making an issue of it. One can wonder whether the air war in the north would have received as much emphasis as it did if there had been a single United States Commander in Vietnam.

Within Vietnam, Westmoreland had three different command relationships with which to concern himself: first, United States government of Vietnam; second, United States civil and military relationships; and finally, control of the fighting forces themselves.

When United States forces were being committed in 1965, a high-level debate arose in Washington as to whether some kind of combined U.S.–G.V.N. command should be formed. The idea had been raised by General H. K. Johnson, Army Chief of Staff, after he returned from a trip to Vietnam. The proposal was not unlike arrangements in the Korean War, where the United States Commander in fact commanded all of the fighting forces. If adopted, the concept would have given the commander—presumably Westmoreland—far greater freedom in deploying forces, rather than requiring constant coordination with Vietnamese counterparts whose motives were ambiguous. When subsequently queried on the matter, however, Westmoreland opposed any merger of commands with the South Vietnamese, primarily because of Vietnamese sensitivities—Ky, and Thieu had publicly come out against the notion. Most senior United States officials in Vietnam felt the South Vietnamese government would never accept United States operational control of their forces, so the notion was never pushed in Saigon. Many now feel that had the Vietnamese forces been placed under United States command, they would have developed into a much more effective force. We will never know.

The United States effort itself consisted of a series of disparate organizations, all of which were in constant contact with their own agencies in Washington. In addition to the military and the embassy, there were such civilian agencies as the United States Information Agency, the United States Agency for International Development, and the Central Intelligence Agency. All of the Ambassadors—Lodge, Taylor, Lodge again, and then Bunker—tried to get consistent and coordinated performance, but they all failed. The Mission Council, established by Ambassador Taylor and composed of top United States officials in Vietnam, was a step in the direction of a cohesive effort, but it was a very small step. Robert Thompson, among others, felt the United States needed a proconsul. My own guess is that this would have worked only if Westmoreland had received the kind of powers Eisenhower had in World War II, which would have eliminated the "business as usual" embassy and replaced it with political advisers to COMUS-MACV.

Finally, there was the problem of command and control of the fighting forces themselves. Faced with the lack of overall command of the military, Westmoreland used the concept of the Tactical Area of Responsibility (TAOR)—one that was originally developed between the United States Marines and South Vietnamese forces. The concept was pragmatic, and appropriate for a war in which there were no front lines and in which military operations took place throughout the country. Specific geographic areas were assigned to specific units, who then had exclusive authority and responsibility to operate within them. A unit could not operate in another unit's TAOR without the permission of its commander.

To provide guidance to units on how to operate in their areas, Westmoreland, and later Abrams, depended on written directives and personal visits to the field. An early directive in September 1965 had the purpose of providing "command policy guidance for orientation of commanders and staffs, and for use in planning and conduct of operations." From time to time campaign plans jointly agreed to by United States and Vietnamese officials were published. They went beyond basic guidance and set forth general objectives for particular time periods. I once asked a United States Corps level commander how he felt about a recently published campaign plan. His response: "I never read them, it would only confuse me."

Westmoreland attempted to control ground operations from his own headquarters, for a variety of reasons. The Vietnamese Joint General Staff, at the level of Westmoreland's headquarters, had no Army component; hence he felt the requirement to coordinate American ground operations at the same level as the Vietnamese. Another reason concerned the interrelated political-military nature of operations, which he felt could more feasibly be controlled at his level. He did in fact at one point want a single field command to control United States ground operations throughout Vietnam. However, this was unacceptable to the United States Marines (since the commander would have been a United States Army General), and the Commander in Chief Pacific, an Admiral, turned the notion down.

COMUSMACV had an almost impossible task in trying to control this diverse war from Saigon. The reaction one gets from those responsible for running the war shows a curious dichotomy between those at division and corps level on the one hand and those below division on the other. First, let us see the response on the questionnaire to a question about operational command and control:

Command and control was	Percentage
(1) About right	57
(2) Should have been more central control—too many units going their own way	3
(3) There was overcontrol of units by higher commanders	35
(4) Other or no answer	5

One general who commanded both a division and a Field Force (corps) commented: "No complaints on command and control. I never had any interference on operations. Each commander was forced to operate by exception and could only operate on crises. At field force level, the span of control was unmanageable." Another division commander: "I was amazed that running the war was left entirely to division commanders. There were no objectives, but there were constraints."

Looking at operations below division level, one gets an entirely different picture. Numerous writers have commented on how lower-level commanders were besieged by battalion, brigade, and even division commanders, ever present in their helicopters, trying to influence the action from the vantage point of 1,500 feet in the air.[26]

The 35 percent of the generals who thought there was overcontrol were, judging by their added comments, thinking of this phenomenon. Typical commentary was: "Too many squad leaders in the sky." "A poor platoon leader with Company, Battalion, Brigade, and Division Commanders in helicopters giving advice. Horrible." One general summed up his thoughts on command and control this way: "At Division level and below, too much focus on small actions. At Corps and higher, not enough mission guidance to subordinate elements."

Interservice Cooperation

The great interservice debates of the 1950's, brought on by the scramble for dollars under the tight Eisenhower defense budgets, decreased greatly with the increased defense funding of the Kennedy and Johnson administrations. The war in Vietnam further eased the pressure for the services to compete for tight dollars. Nevertheless, there was some interservice controversy during the course of the war.

For a period of about ten years prior to the United States intervention, there had been a conflict between the Army and the Air Force over air transport and close firepower support for Army combat units. As operations increased in Vietnam, the realities of the combat situation soon caused both Army and Air Force officers to adjust major differences in outlook, but not before the Chairman JCS and COMUSMACV themselves became involved.

Leaving aside the technical details, the Air Force argument was that the Army, under the guise of an air assault division, was set-

26. See, for example, Zeb B. Bradford, Jr., and Frederic J. Brown, *The United States Army in Transition* (Beverly Hills, Sage Publications, 1973), pp. 236, 237; and Mylander, *The Generals*, pp. 194, 195.

ting up its own air force and undercutting the United States Air force. On the one hand, the Army had invaded the transport role with both fixed wing and helicopter aircraft, and on the other, the Army helicopter gunships were invading the close fire-support role of the Air Force. The discussion was so heated in 1964 that General Wheeler feared the possibility of a Congressional investigation of roles and missions and the use of air power. In the end, the Army kept its helicopters (transport and fire support) and gave a small fixed-wing transport called the Caribou to the Air Force.

Another problem for the Air Force was who would be Westmoreland's Deputy Commander. Westmoreland took the position that it was a ground war, and since the enemy had no air force, his Deputy should be an Army general. General Moore, Air Force Commander in Vietnam early in the intervention, was under constant pressure from higher Air Force officials to obtain a greater role and enhanced prestige for the Air Force in Vietnam. At one point he received a tongue-lashing from the Air Force Chief of Staff, Curtis Lemay, for not pushing the Air Force role enough. Matters eased up after Lemay retired in 1965.

Compromise was reached on the issue of the Deputy COMUS-MACV, and Westmoreland kept his ground Deputy. Eventually, among others, Abrams and Weyand, successors to Westmoreland's job, filled this position. In addition, an Air Deputy was appointed who was also the Air Commander in Vietnam. He functioned not as an alter ego to Westmoreland but as a Deputy concerned only with Air Force matters.

Army controversies with the Marines were somewhat more heated and continued for a longer period of time. Marine General David Shoup, writing from retirement in the April 1969 *Atlantic*, stated that much of the loss of credibility of the Johnson Administration over the reporting of the war had as its basis its "gamesmanship" of the interservice contest. He referred also to Marine planners long waiting for an "acceptable excuse to thrust a landing force" into Vietnam to provide continued justification for the Marine amphibious function. Westmoreland himself noted how anxious the Marines were to "break a record" getting ashore, once they received the word to land in 1965.

Once they were in Vietnam, Westmoreland also detected a tendency for the Marine chain of command outside of Vietnam to influence unduly the tactical conduct of Marine forces under his operational command. He observed what he felt was a major campaign by the Marines in Washington to promote themselves as being the most effective element in the Vietnam conflict. The commander in Vietnam was not the only one concerned with Marine ambitions: the Army staff in Washington was almost paranoid on the subject. In 1966 the operations staff informed the Army Chief of Staff that they thought the Marines might advance the argument that their forces were uniquely suited to the Mekong Delta in an attempt to justify the addition of a Marine Division to their worldwide force.

Marine tactics sometimes came in for their share of criticism. Marines early took a great interest in pacification and civil action and used considerable of their assets in this way. Certain members of the MACV staff, though not objecting to pacification activities, felt nevertheless that the Marines should give greater attention to search-and-destroy operations. Westmoreland was persuaded in November 1965 to send the commander of the Marine Amphibious Force a letter which in effect requested that he conduct offensive operations of the search-and-destroy type with greater frequency. The letter was interpreted as a directive but was also couched in negotiation terms typical of the war in Vietnam—that is to say, "I would like to see a plan," etc., rather than the "you will" characteristic of the Korean War or World War II.

The biggest controversy that Westmoreland became involved in with the Marines concerned their aviation. Each Marine Division had its own dedicated air wing—good for the division but expensive in resources. The Air Force operated on the principle of theater control of air operations as being economically most desirable as well as permitting concentration of airpower at the most decisive points at any given time. Westmoreland, who had operational control of the Air Force in Vietnam and of the Marines (but not their air element directly), was in the middle of these differing views and was responsible for the outcome of all operations.

As early as 1966 MACV studied the possibility of giving the Air Force Commander in Vietnam operational control of the Marine aircraft. This would have permitted him to remove Marine air wings from their own divisions and employ them elsewhere if, in his opinion, the situation required such a reallocation. A compromise solution was arrived at in which the Marines provided a certain number of sorties each day, to be allocated by the Air

Force. Any major change, MACV felt, "would arouse a violent and emotional opposition on the part of the Marines at every echelon from Vietnam to the White House."

In the end this opposition did in fact materialize, brought about by actions of Westmoreland just before and during the Communist Tet 1968 offensive. The immediate problem was the redeployment of the Army's 1st Cavalry Division to Thua Thien province in the north, where Air Force support was not adequate. Westmoreland expressed the opinion to the Marine Commander General Cushman and the Marine Air Commander General Anderson that a single management of air power was necessary in the circumstances. In the course of the conversation, Anderson became rather "emotional," declaring that the Marine air wing belonged to the Marines and no one else.

The situation was not resolved satisfactorily and took an inordinate amount of Westmoreland's time. The best that was achieved was a single tactical air-control system run by the Air Force, which at least kept the air assets sorted out. Meanwhile, however, Westmoreland's efforts generated a big interservice fight in the Pentagon, led by Marine Commandant Leonard Chapman, which eventually reached the President. LBJ raised the subject later with Westmoreland, who explained the problem to the President's satisfaction. Still, the Marines did retain control of their air assets.[27]

There was less interaction between Army and Navy than between the Army and the other services. The Naval Commander in Vietnam under Westmoreland's operational command provided effective coastal surveillance to prevent enemy supplies from being landed and managed the naval portion of the Riverine Force. This was a mobile force operating in the delta for a period of two years and composed of elements of the Navy and the Army's 9th Division. Although service differences did arise from time to time, pragmatic solutions were worked out by those immediately involved. The other Navy war—of carriers, cruisers, etc.—was a Navy war completely. These vessels were part of the Seventh Fleet and operated through a Navy chain of command. Had Westmoreland been a theater commander, he would have had operational control of these forces also. It was quite clear from the early days of the war on, however, that the Navy was not going to let that happen.

27. See Westmoreland, *A Soldier Reports*, pp. 342, 345.

The war managers were specifically asked questions about inter-service cooperation with the following results:

Interservice Cooperation with	Air Force	Marines	Navy
(1) Outstanding	60%	22%	29%
(2) Adequate but could be improved	37	43	45
(3) Not satisfactory, big improvement needed	2	17	13
(4) No answer	1	16	12
(5) Other	0	2	1

The large number not answering the Navy and Marine questions no doubt reflects the fact that many Army generals did not work closely with either of those services, whereas almost all had direct contact with the Air Force. It is interesting that many generals who worked most closely with the Marines praised them highly in their added commentary. Perhaps the problem lay elsewhere. One senior general in a position to know commented: "The trouble was with the Marine Headquarters in Washington and Marine Headquarters Pacific, not in Vietnam."

VC/NVA Strategy and Tactics

There is considerable question whether in fighting the war in South Vietnam the United States ever really understood the enemy. In retrospect, Westmoreland thinks not. In fact, he views the inability to understand the motivations and perspective of the enemy and his method of operations as "the basic error" in the conduct of the war in South Vietnam.

Maxwell Taylor has written of the early difficulty of obtaining good information on the enemy in South Vietnam as he observed it during his 1961 visit.[28] Robert Komer is even more specific, pointing out that the basic intelligence needed was alien to the United States and GVN intelligence apparatus, which was focused to too great an extent on enemy main force units at the expense of information on the local guerrillas or the Viet Cong infrastructure. As a result, Komer says, we failed to understand that the enemy's goals

28. Taylor, pp. 236–239.

were as political as they were military, and we erroneously concluded that we were doing much better in our efforts against the
Viet Cong than in reality we were.[29] The discussion that follows
concerning the enemy's strategy and tactics, and the enemy himself, is, of course, retrospective and therefore does not represent
the way he was viewed at any one point in the war.

The basic strategy of the Viet Cong and North Vietnamese was
derived from Mao's "People's War"—a term he applied to the
political-military strategy he developed in the long fight against the
Kuomintang and the Japanese, and through which he achieved
control of China in 1949. The primary objective of the strategy in
Vietnam, as in China, was control of the people in the countryside.
As this control increased, the official government was restricted
increasingly to the cities and to the major routes of communications. The eventual goal was to achieve enough strength to capture
the cities and overthrow the government. A key aspect of the insurgency was the political infrastructure, which was central to the
political-military effort. At each level, the military element of the
Viet Cong was subordinate to the political element.

At the grass-roots level, the military were part-time soldier-
guerrillas. At the district and province level, the Viet Cong forces
were called "local forces," who stayed generally within their own
geographic areas. At higher levels came the Viet Cong (and subsequently North Vietnamese) main force units. These were organized into separate regiments and divisions. Unlike the local
forces, these units were moved anywhere in the country, or out of
it into sanctuaries. The VC military at all levels were not only subordinate to the political, but also dependent on it for recruitment,
supplies, and intelligence.

Without underestimating the great sacrifices and efforts of the
Viet Cong, the insurgency in the South and especially the orches-
tration of the overall military-political effort was controlled by the
North, certainly from 1959 onward. In 1959 cadres who had moved
north in 1954 began to return to the South. After 1963 there was an
increased movement to the South of North Vietnamese Army
units, and the Tet Offensive of 1968 was planned in the North.

In the view of the North Vietnamese leadership, there were
three main tasks: First, to permit the insurgency in the South to
survive. To accomplish this, increasing North Vietnamese forces
had to be committed. Second, to develop support for the Viet Cong

29. Komer, pp. 59, 60.

among the South Vietnamese population that was uncommitted, with the use of any instrument, including terror. Third, there was the target of American public opinion; from the time the first demonstrations in the United States against the war began in late 1965, it was perceived that a hostile political reaction to the war could be developed.

Certainly there were divergencies among the North Vietnamese leaders about how best to accomplish these objectives. For our purpose, one of the more interesting of these was General Vo Nguyen Giap, Defense Minister and a member of the Politburo. During the course of the war, he made a number of pronouncements stressing the importance of political-military coordination and emphasizing the protracted nature of the war.

His major pronouncement, which he called "Big Victory, Great Task," was published in a military newspaper in the fall of 1967. In this article Giap reviewed the war up to that point and prescribed the strategy he thought best suited to defeat the United States. His main stress was on the actions of small units, but he called also for the use of large main-force units when such appeared with widespread, small-unit actions while concentrating major units on carefully selected targets. Coming at the time it did, this pronouncement has been read as a warning to his colleagues against the Tet 1968 offensive, planning for which was already well under way.

In any case, Giap's subsequent speeches in late 1968 and mid-1969 reiterated his 1967 thesis regarding a long drawn-out war during which presumably American public opinion would force United States troop withdrawal and permit in time a climactic battle against the forces of South Vietnam—both of which subsequently occurred. As Giap viewed the United States position, he felt its global commitments and eroding domestic base would prevent any significant deployment of additional troops after 1967. Since by that time the United States had been denied an all-out rapid victory, the war would grind on as a protracted and frustrating one which Americans were ill-equipped to conduct. Central to the success of North Vietnamese strategy was the ability to accept the casualties which the United States war of attrition imposed.

From the enemy viewpoint, then, an important question was the extent to which he could control his casualties. The answer appears to have been based upon his ability to avoid contact with Free World forces, when he wished to avoid such contact. Empirically, it seems in retrospect that the enemy was able to choose the time and place of most of his fire fights. On many occasions one heard of United States forces being unable to find the enemy. And when he did elect to fight, he usually chose—Tet 1968 being an obvious exception—the most favorable battlefield conditions open to him.

The ability to control casualties was an integral part of the overall enemy strategy in Vietnam. His attacks were designed to have maximum psychological impact by inflicting, if possible, heavy United States or South Vietnamese casualties and projecting at the same time the impression of strength throughout South Vietnam.

The question arises how the enemy was able to accept the casualties he did, considering his relatively small population base. The answer is that his casualties never reached the point where he could not sustain them. No doubt, labor requirements caused by the war imposed some strain, but they seem always to have been offset by normal population growth and by employing marginal elements of the work force.

In effect, then, the United States strategy of attrition was a failure on two levels. First, an attrition strategy is a test of wills, and in this regard the enemy will proved superior. Second, since the enemy had the initiative, he was able to control the number of casualties and always to keep that number within the limits he could afford. The rate of attrition was capable of being sustained by the enemy for many years longer than the United States will to continue.

To replace their casualties, the North Vietnamese had to maintain an elaborate infiltration system down the jungle trails from North Vietnam into Laos and Cambodia and finally into South Vietnam. Replacement groups took anywhere from one to five months to move into South Vietnam, depending on the location to which they were traveling. In the process, there were losses from disease and United States firepower. However, the North Vietnamese were determined to make the system work, and it did.

Conditions for travel were better from November through April, and therefore the majority of infiltrators started southward during these months. The rate varied to meet operational needs in the South, and sometimes heavy infiltration was continued into the summer. The logistics supply system was equally difficult to maintain, except for a substantial period when logistic support for a large portion of South Vietnam was delivered by boat to Sihanoukville and trucked up to the border areas.

The United States enemy in Vietnam was technologically primitive, able to endure hardship, and determined to make his political-military strategy work despite the casualties he suffered. What did the United States Army general officers think of their opponents? There were two survey questions related to the capability of enemy forces. The question concerning the VC was directed toward the period prior to the Tet 1968 offensive, since the casualties of that force were so great during the offensive that the VC were greatly weakened thereafter.

Capability of the VC prior to Tet '68	*Percentage*
(1) Skilled and tough fighters	57
(2) Adequate fighters	33
(3) Left something to be desired as fighters	6
(4) No answer	4

Capability of the Army of NVN	
(1) A skilled and tough force	44
(2) An adequate force	32
(3) A force that left something to be desired	23
(4) Other	1

Additional commentary by the generals was not extensive. There was some indication that the North Vietnamese forces had slowly improved, while the Viet Cong declined after Tet 1968. Here are some interesting, though admittedly not typical, comments:

The CIA told us we could not lick those people, but that had policy implications beyond intelligence analysis and estimates.

One underlying assumption that was erroneous was that a demonstration of intent would cause the other side to fall back. The civilian leadership especially took this position.

The North Vietnamese were effective because of determination. In a technical sense, they were not so good and were used as cannon fodder by their leadership.

Giap could have gone on indefinitely. It was unwinnable the way we played it.

There was a tendency to underestimate the enemy. They were in fact the best enemy we have faced in our history. Tenacious and physically fit. How they did it needs study.

Measuring Progress

When the United States presence began to develop in Vietnam in 1954–59, there was no central coordinating agency, and each activity was reported back through its own channels to Washington. The Military Advisory Group, which was the predecessor of Military Assistance Command, concentrated.on reporting on progress in developing the South Vietnamese forces. The reporting during the 1950's was generally unsystematic, which seemed to cause no problems until the situation began to deteriorate about 1960.

The Kennedy Administration's interest in what was going on resulted, among other things, in General Maxwell Taylor's trip there in 1961. In his report to the President on the trip, he stressed the need to improve the quality of the information being gathered, so that Washington could make a better assessment of progress by the Vietnamese in what was by now clearly a war.[30]

Action followed recommendation and the Advisory Group became an Assistance Command with its own intelligence staff. Progress in reporting was slow to improve, but as the number of United States advisers went from under 1,000 to about 10,000 during 1962, the basis for a reporting system became available throughout the country. The chief weakness was that the advisers for many reasons were dependent on their Vietnamese counterparts for the information they reported back. The result was an overoptimistic approach to reporting on the part of both Vietnamese and Americans in an effort to meet goals, at least on paper. Some of this optimism was challenged in Washington and by a very few reporters in Vietnam, such as Neil Sheehan and David Halberstam.

In the generally depressed situation in Vietnam after the November 1963 coup against Diem, it became evident that reports of progress had been very misleading. In *The Lost Crusade*, Chester Cooper tells of heading a small interdepartmental team to Saigon in March 1964 to look into the reporting system.[31] The efforts of this group, combined with others, resulted in a pacification reporting system which survived for two years. We will consider this and subsequent developments in pacification reporting in Chapter 4.

Meanwhile, the MACV J-3 (Operations) was developing a re-

30. Taylor, chap. 18.
31. Cooper, *The Lost Crusade*, p. 229.

porting system of its own, along with J-2 (Intelligence), consisting of quantitative data on military indicators of progress. These included body counts, weapons captured, friendly sorties flown, and many other items. Since the war was soon to become one of attrition, the body count, to which we will return shortly, was regarded as one of the most important indicators of progress. Because of the difficulty in measuring the results of the employment of air and artillery, the measurement of progress here became output rather than results—the number of missions flown or rounds of artillery delivered, for example. An external reason why these statistics became so important was the well-known proclivity of Secretary of Defense McNamara to deal in statistics, which resulted in an attempt to measure all progress in absolute terms.

By the time the American intervention was well under way in 1965 and 1966, the means appeared to exist for a full-fledged American reporting system, through its own channels, on progress in the war. These reports were brought together under the overall rubric of the Measurement of Progress system. Before explaining the system, it is worth considering why the war in Vietnam was so difficult to grasp militarily.

The previous mainstay in the measurement of progress in conventional warfare had been the main line of resistance—that is to say, the line of contact between opposing forces. In World War II, for example, if the invasion plan called for Allied forces to be on the line of the Seine River by 120 days after the Normandy landing, then progress or lack thereof could be visualized on the ground. However, the war in Vietnam was nonlinear: there was no main line of resistance. Some substitute had to be devised to measure progress in a guerrilla war.

The Measurement of Progress system can be described by using one of its monthly reports with which I happen to be familiar. The data contained in these reports were sent through normal United States military channels up to the Military Assistance Command. The report of June 1967 in slide form came to some seventy-one transparencies. It included strength and strength trends of the opposing forces; efforts of friendly forces in sorties; the percentage of time that battalions spent on various types of missions (the United States that month spent 86 percent of its battalion time on search and destroy missions); enemy base areas neutralized; enemy losses; and the degree of government control of roads, population, etc.

The report concluded with the following summarized statistics:

Enemy base areas 37% neutralized, a decrease of 13% from previous month.

Roads adequately secured 86%, an increase of 1% from previous month.

Waterways 12% secure, a decrease of 5% from previous month.

Population controlled by government 61%.

Attrition of enemy manpower was greater than his new input of manpower for the first time.

The written summary that followed did not put undue emphasis on progress during the previous month. In time, these reports became more sophisticated and other measures were used, but this example gives the general idea.

What were these reports used for? More than one would imagine, given their relatively crude basis. When Westmoreland was COMUSMACV, he was briefed monthly on this report in front of his assembled staff officers. This was a time for some reflection on overall management of the war, and frequently at these sessions Westmoreland instructed his staff on future operations. Usually, within a week of the staff briefing, he would hold a meeting of his principal commanders at which the Measurement of Progress briefing was one of the agenda items. That the United States Commander placed great faith in these reports and statistics is also attested by other uses he made of them.

In late April 1967 Westmoreland addressed a joint session of the United States Congress on the situation in Vietnam. The address was about five pages in length and about two thirds of a page was taken up with statistics from the report. Secretary McNamara—for whose benefit, no doubt, the report was partially conceived—frequently received the briefing (in different form) on his visits to Vietnam.

One memorable visit was McNamara's trip to Saigon in July 1967 when another request for more troops, which eventually became Program 5, was being discussed. Because of the June war in the Middle East, the trip had been postponed. For two to three weeks the briefers used the statistics from the progress report in work on the briefing. The objective was to get the briefing into a statistical format convincing to McNamara. General Westmoreland, General Abrams, who was by now Deputy COMUSMACV, and Ambassador Komer, in charge of the United States pacification effort, served as the "murder board." Slides changed, rationales were rearranged, and so on, night and day. Finally the big day came and McNamara said he was impressed. Subsequently a small increase in troop strength was approved, though not to the level requested. The day of McNamara's briefing was July 6, 1967, the same day the North Vietnamese leadership began meeting in Hanoi to plan their Tet 1968 offensive.

Even the President was not immune from the Saigon statistics. In November 1967 both General Westmoreland and Ambassador Bunker were back in Washington giving LBJ an optimistic report on the war. In the briefing they managed to get in the kill ratios along with fifteen or so other indicators. By now, the State and Pentagon bureaucracies were highly skeptical both of the validity of certain of the statistics on which these reports were based, and of the analysis itself from which Saigon was drawing its optimistic conclusions. This skepticism was not getting through to the President, however.

The statistical approach was a way of coming to grips with a problem that by 1967 had become serious. Time was running out, not for the insurgents but for the patience of the American people, because the Administration was not able to produce a credible and coherent report on progress in the war. Some observers felt that one of the problems was precisely that officials on the levels of Bunker and Westmoreland were engaging in detailed discussion of matters they did not fully understand. An alternative approach would have been for the ambassadors and senior generals to confine themselves to policy statements, while at the same time allowing greater freedom of discussion between the press and field personnel.

Some of the criticism by the Washington bureaucracy had to do with the nature of the military reporting system itself. Reports from different sources seemed not to agree. Results were, it was suspected, sometimes faked, since certain of the reporters were grading their own progress. When higher commanders rode lower ones for better statistical results, it was evident that they were going to get either the statistics or the results, and on fortunate occasions both.

The interpretation of statistics also left open some questions. For

example, there was the issue of neutralizing enemy base camps.
What precisely did it mean that 37 percent of the base camps were
neutralized at any one time? Could not the enemy subsequently
return or build new ones in the endless jungles, the critics asked.
Another criticism was that quality or costs were usually not shown
along with results. For example, to say that a certain highway was
cleared for use did not indicate the quantity, quality, or frequency
of traffic that could move on a road. Nor did it give the cost in
resources to keep the road open. In other words, if a particular
road was open, how important was it—considering the opportunity
costs, since resources were always limited?

Perhaps the most serious criticism of the measurements of progress was that in aggregate they did not really tell how the war was
going. Granted their relevance to the military aspects of the war,
but was not this a political war with political objectives? Although
the military aspects had to be addressed and required substantial
resources, so the argument went, were they not secondary? If the
primary purpose of the insurgents was to undermine the South
Vietnamese government by demonstrating it was unable to maintain stability, then it was not necessary at this stage for them to
defeat the government forces decisively. Their only problem was to
keep from getting defeated fully and to outlast the government and
its American supporters. At a later stage the government would
either have collapsed or the Americans would have gone, and then
the government forces could be defeated in the classical military
sense. As regards the statistical system, then, measurements of
success on the military side were important but in aggregate could
not in themselves lead to an overall assessment of progress.

The chief critics of analysis made in Saigon were in McNamara's
Systems Analysis Office, which published a document entitled
"Southeast Asia Analysis Report." This was an unofficial report and
was very frank in its criticisms. Although many thought it served a
useful purpose, the Chairman of the Joint Chiefs was not one of
them. On one occasion he recommended to the Secretary of Defense that the report, which was widely disseminated, be limited to
the Secretary's staff.

When all else is forgotten about statistical reporting in the
Vietnamese War, the body count will be remembered. This particular statistical report had its origins in the early 1960's in an
effort to give credibility to claims by the South Vietnamese of hav-

ing killed a certain number of enemy in a particular action. Soon advisers began to report the number of friendly and enemy losses in a particular engagement. The idea was that the bodies of the enemy were to be actually counted—not estimated—and that would induce the press, for example, to accept the claims. The irony was that as a new generation of reporters came along, they took issue with the crudeness of the practice and at the same time questioned the validity of the reports themselves.

By the time the American intervention was under way, the figures were being aggregated in reports by month and year. The Measurement of Progress Report, for instance, showed absolute kills as well as kill ratios. In time some units used it as their central measurement yardstick, and inevitably headquarters began to compare units' effectiveness by their kill ratios and body counts. I can recall my astonishment, on returning to Vietnam in the spring of 1969 and attending my first evening briefing at II Field Force, to note that the first seven charts concerned body count and kill ratio: this unit compared with that unit; this year compared with last year; night compared with day, and so on.

Critics of these measurements felt that they told very little. Kill ratio was meaningful only if a continuously favorable ratio meant that the enemy could no longer sustain such an adverse ratio. Actually, since he did not concern himself with the ratio, the real test was his will to sustain the absolute losses and go on fighting, and the same obtained for the Americans and South Vietnamese. Whose will eventually prevailed, we all know now.

As for the body count itself, it could mean one of two things: either the enemy was increasing his military effort and there was no way of stopping him, or we were being very successful in defeating him. Moreover, there was no way of really comparing the number of enemy against his manpower potential because the manpower base varied with the effectiveness of his political apparatus and losses never approached his absolute limit to sustain them.

Body count had its defenders, and one of the best known is Lieutenant General Julian J. Ewell. Ewell was an army brat who graduated from West Point in 1939. He was one of the early parachutists and jumped into Normandy on D-Day as part of the 101st Airborne Division. He became a colonel less than six years out of West Point, but did not become brigadier general until 1963. In the Vietnam War he commanded the 9th Infantry Divi-

sion and later II Field Force. He was the General Lemming of
Josiah Bunting's novel of the war, *The Lionheads*. He devised
many statistical methods for managing the war; for his officers, the
most controversial were those concerning the body count. An aggressive and decisive officer, Ewell was an excellent tactician. He
spoke with a country twang and was known for the caustic way in
which he transmitted instructions.

Ewell's defense of the body count is set forth in an Army monograph.[32] Basically, he contends that the system was one of the few
ways to get a handle on the war—to be certain that resources were
efficiently employed. Furthermore, he maintains that this emphasis need not have led to civilian casualties if training and controls had been carried out.

There is another level of criticism of the body count approach,
however: the charge that it led to shoddy practices. A high body
count, it was alleged, became a career necessity for ambitious
officers and led to falsification of reports, sapping the integrity of
the officers corps in the process.[33] More serious allegations concern
the unnecessary civilian and United States military casualties in-
curred by going after a high body count.[34]

There were three survey questions on the measurement of progress in the war, with the following results:

The Measurement of Progress system with all its
indicators   *Percentage*
   (1) Was a valid system to measure progress in the war   2
   (2) Valid to a point but should have been used more
      as a management tool than to measure progress   62
   (3) Not a valid way to measure progress in the war   32
   (4) Other or no answer   4

One important indicator was kill ratio. Was this
   (1) A valuable indicator and necessary in managing
      the war   4
   (2) A rough device that was better than others   35
   (3) A misleading device to estimate progress   55
   (4) Other or no answer   6

32. Lt. Gen. Julian J. Ewell and Maj. Gen. Ira A. Hunt, Jr., *Sharpening the Combat Edge* (Washington, Government Printing Office, 1974),
pp. 227–228.
33. Mylander, pp. 80–82.
34. King, pp. 25, 28, 30, 101.

The kill ratio was based upon body count. Was body count
   (1) Within reason accurate   26
   (2) Underestimated   3
   (3) Often inflated   61
   (4) Other or no answer   10

As might be expected, the third question brought forth a torrent
of comment from the generals, and I will quote more extensively
here because their comments give considerable insight into the
thinking of this group.

The immensity of the false reporting is a blot on the honor of
the Army.

The bane of my existence and just about got me fired as a
division commander. They were grossly exaggerated by many
units primarily because of the incredible interest shown by
people like McNamara and Westmoreland. I shudder to think
how many of our soldiers were killed on a body-counting
mission—what a waste.

A fake—totally worthless.

A great crime and cancer in the Army in the eyes of young
officers in 1969–1971.

Gruesome—a ticket-punching item.

Often blatant lies.

General X was particularly guilty and I told him so.

I had one Division Commander whose reports I never believed or trusted.

Many commanders resorted to false reports to prevent their
own relief.

It should be appended that a significant amount of commentary
stressed two points. First, the validity of the reporting varied
greatly between units and depended on the position of the commander, especially the Division Commander. Secondly, South
Vietnamese units were much more likely to exaggerate body count
than American units.

The Tet Offensive

The Tet Offensive of early 1968 was the high point of military action in the Second Indochinese War. After all other specific battles have been forgotten, it will be remembered. It was a watershed, and afterward nothing was ever quite the same in the war. Although a military defeat for the VC/NVA in a technical sense, it was a tremendous psychological victory for them in the United States. In part, this was due to the optimistic expectations that the American people had developed on the basis of the pronouncements of their own civilian and military leadership, including the leadership in Vietnam.

That an enemy attack was staged was not a surprise to the American leadership in Saigon. What was a surprise was the scope and magnitude of the attack when it came. In the first days of October 1967, General Westmoreland was cabling Washington that the enemy had made some serious decisions. He hypothesized that the enemy was feeling the effects of the attrition strategy and had perhaps decided on a maximum effort over a short period of time.

Still other comments by Westmoreland indicated that the war had reached its penultimate stage and would end in victory for the United States. Speaking to the National Press Club in Washington on November 21, 1967, the United States Commander indicated that by the beginning of the new year the war would enter Phase III, its next to last phase. Although the phase was not defined in terms of an overall objective, the fifteen objectives listed would, if accomplished, place the South Vietnamese Government in a position to begin to take over the management of the war by itself. In other statements, COMUSMACV implied that Phase III would take about two years to complete.

Upon his return to Vietnam, General Westmoreland announced twenty-five goals to be accomplished by his command in the year 1968. These included making ineffective all of the enemy's main force units and inflicting casualties on enemy units faster than they could be replaced. His forces were indeed to render many enemy units ineffective but not in the manner or with the outcome planned.

Not all observers of Vietnam in late 1967 were equally sanguine about the new year. David Halberstam, writing in the December *Harper's*, drew opposite conclusions from Westmoreland. "I do not," he wrote, "think we are winning in any true sense, nor do I see any true signs that we are about to win." He reflected the thoughts of a growing number of Americans, private and public, who knew far less about the situation than Westmoreland or his generals.

The bubble broke in the early morning hours of January 30, 1968. As the reports of enemy attacks began to pour into MACV, followed by reports of an even greater number of attacks on the following two days, it was evident that an enemy effort of major proportions was under way. Essentially simultaneous attacks (there were understandably some problems in coordination) took place in over one hundred cities and towns, including Saigon, where the American Embassy was briefly under siege. What, the American people wondered, was happening? Were we not supposed to be winning? How could an attack of such proportions be initiated by an enemy we were defeating?

Actually, the Tet Offensive was a tremendous military defeat for the Viet Cong and the North Vietnamese. Nowhere, for very long, could they carve out defensible areas, and there was no general uprising by the South Vietnamese population. The Viet Cong were able to hold on here and there until late February, finally being cleared out of Hue by the 25th of the month. With that the tactical aspects of the Tet Offensive had run their course.

Friendly losses had been high, about 6,000 killed, and enemy losses were staggering. No one knows for certain, but perhaps they reached 40,000. The Viet Cong, who bore the brunt of the action, lost the best of a generation of guerrillas, and thereafter had to be replaced increasingly by North Vietnamese.

The South Vietnamese Government and forces held and gained enough political strength to achieve their first real mobilization. The American public, however, who were the key to the problem, did not hold. The psychological impact on a nation that thought itself to be winning was too great. It was obvious that popular support for the war no longer existed, and this was confirmed on March 31, when President Johnson removed himself as a possible candidate for President in 1968. All of this has been chronicled ably elsewhere, and need not detain us.[35] However, there are further relevant points to consider, in viewing the war from the perspective of its general officer managers.

There is, first, the case of the Khe Sanh outpost astride Highway 9 near the Laotian border in the northern part of South Vietnam. Originally established as a patrol base for blocking infiltration routes, the outpost became a symbol of the American effort by the time of the Tet Offensive. By late December 1967 it was evident that enemy forces were massing in the vicinity of the base for the presumed purpose of overrunning it.

Soon the base came under constant siege and in fact no longer was effective in blocking infiltration. However, its real purpose by this time was to support conventional operations into Laos, should such operations be approved in Washington. They never were for American forces. (The South Vietnamese incursion into Laos in early 1971 will be discussed in a later chapter.) In any case, Khe Sanh received enormous attention and very effective support by the Air Force in terms of supply and employment of B-52 bombardment. The cable traffic between Washington and Saigon in early 1968 referred to the possibility that Giap intended to make it another Dien Bien Phu. At one point, President Johnson extracted public pledges from the Joint Chiefs that it was both important and could be successfully defended.

In time Khe Sanh was evacuated, although it was then no longer under siege. Meanwhile, it had tied up over 5,000 Marines plus other potential relief forces who some say could have been used elsewhere during the Tet Offensive.[36] Perhaps in part this was its purpose. Robert Thompson holds the position that Giap in any case would never have overrun the outpost even if he could have, since it would have had the effect of strenghtening the faltering resolve of the American public to continue the war.[37]

If what happened at Khe Sanh had no real effect on the outcome of the war, another military decision made during the Tet Offensive had a very important one on its future conduct. This was the decision by General Westmoreland and General Wheeler to re-

35. An interesting and readable account of the Tet Offensive and its significance is Dan Oberdorfer, *Tet* (New York, Doubleday, 1971). Westmoreland tells his own story of Tet in *A Soldier Reports*, chap. 17.

36. It can be argued alternatively that it kept an estimated 14,000 North Vietnamese tied up in the siege.

37. Thompson, *No Exit from Vietnam*, pp. 68–70.

quest 206,000 additional forces. The request brought about a review in Washington of where we were heading in Vietnam—with profound results.

Shortly after the start of the Tet Offensive, Wheeler, by message, was encouraging COMUSMACV to ask for what he felt he needed in the way of forces to cope with the new situation. Westmoreland's thinking along these lines was initially conservative. He cabled Washington that while he could use additional troops, he was not making a firm demand for them, although he did want the arrival of those forces already programmed for Vietnam to be accelerated.

At the request of the President, Chairman Wheeler arrived in Vietnam on February 23 to see the situation at first hand and to confer with Westmoreland.

General Earl G. Wheeler played an important role in Washington decision-making on Vietnam during his tour as Chairman JCS from 1964 to 1970. A West Point graduate in the class of 1932, Wheeler's climb was based on his superb skills as a staff officer, his commands being only incidental. He came through as gentlemanly, urbane, and highly articulate. He understood the Washington bureaucracy, better perhaps than any active duty officer at that time. As the interface between the civilian and military leadership during the Vietnamese war, he had experienced considerable frustrations.

With the coming of the Tet Offensive Wheeler perceived that he had his foot in the door to accomplish something that had troubled him for some time. Specifically, he wished to reconstitute the strategic reserve, which had been depleted by the requirements of Vietnam. This would require the call-up of Reserve Forces which had been previously denied.

With Wheeler's encouragement, during his visit to Saigon, Westmoreland developed a plan for approximately 206,000 additional troops. Of this total, Wheeler would recommend that 100,000 go to Vietnam and the remainder be held in strategic reserve. Whether the latter would ever be sent to Vietnam would depend on separate decisions later.[38] Westmoreland's plan was to

38. A remarkable bit of interviewing of Generals Wheeler and Westmoreland on this matter is in John Henry, "March 1968: Continuity or Change," unpublished honors thesis, Harvard College, Department of Government, 1971.

place the 100,000 troops in the Northern Corps and, if approved, use them for campaigns north of the DMZ and into Laos.

When Westmoreland's request reached the President, it apparently was depicted as somewhat more urgent than the Commander in Saigon viewed it. In any case, what happened thereafter has been told from several conflicting points of view.[39] Clark Clifford, who was designated to replace McNamara as Secretary of Defense on March 1, was asked by the President to look into Westmoreland's request. There was by this time a good deal of skepticism among Washington officials about the course of the war, and the Clifford group, rather than merely look for means to meet the troop request, as in the past, used the request to ask fundamental questions about the conduct of the war itself.

The outcome, as is well known, was that the recommendations of the group to the President were framed in such a manner as to prevent any further escalation of the war. A modest troop increase of under 25,000 was approved and a small Reserve Force call-up was approved. Separately, the President decided to halt bombing in North Vietnam as a stimulus to opening negotiations with the North Vietnamese, which later occurred. All of this was announced by the President in his famous address of March 31, 1968, which concluded with his announcement that he had decided not to seek another term as President.[40]

The Tet Offensive was a dramatic and significant military action which caused the United States to reconsider and alter its strategy in Vietnam. It changed American public opinion in such a way that it led to negotiations, the downfall of a President, and eventually to a plan for United States withdrawal.

In that same month of March, General Westmoreland received word from the President that shortly he would be departing Vietnam to become the Chief of Staff of the United States Army. Apparently McNamara had recommended the change in January, before Tet, and Clifford in March made a similar recommendation. General Creighton W. Abrams, Westmoreland's Deputy and West Point classmate, was named as his successor in Vietnam.

39. Johnson, chap. 11. Clifford, "A Vietnam Reappraisal," pp. 601–622. Townsend Hoopes, *The Limits of Intervention*, passim.

40. During the previous November when Westmoreland was in Washington and a guest in the White House, the President told him confidentially that he had made the decision not to run again. Westmoreland, p. 233.

The Other Wars

For about two years after United States military intervention in Vietnam in 1965, the major attention of those managing the war was directed toward the military effort. Nevertheless, there was always the realization that eventual stabilization of the country depended on adequate and efficient South Vietnamese armed forces and a viable government attuned to the needs of the Vietnamese people. To this end, the United States worked jointly with the South Vietnamese on an advisory effort within the structure of their governmental apparatus. United States efforts in both areas increased with the passage of time, and toward the end of direct American involvement in late 1972 seemed marginally successful—although subsequently this turned out not to be true. The advisory program was a United States military effort and the pacification was a civilian and military effort. At higher levels, however, both were controlled by Army generals and, to a lesser extent, Marine generals. These "other wars," as they were sometimes called, were handled quite differently.

The Advisory Effort

THE SOUTH VIETNAMESE

There were, to begin with, a significant number of attitudinal differences between Americans and South Vietnamese that were difficult for advisers to perceive and even more difficult to take account of in day-to-day operations.[1]

1. I am indebted to Dr. Abraham Hirsch, formerly of USAID, for the attitudinal differences between Vietnamese and Americans. I have made some minor changes on the basis of my own experiences.

The Vietnamese, like other ethnic groups in Southeast Asia, are formalistic, tending to stress how things are done rather than what they are doing. They value tradition for its own sake. This latter point is particularly important because Americans, particularly those in advisory roles, saw themselves as in Vietnam to change the way the Vietnamese did things. This was perceived by some Vietnamese as the efforts of outsiders to change their traditions without understanding them.

Another attitudinal difference between the two cultures is that while we tend to view alternatives as either good or bad, with no shades of gray, the Vietnamese believe that extremes can be reconciled, or can at least coexist. The Vietnamese approach may stress only indirect action, focused, perhaps, on the background of a problem rather than the problem itself.

A third important difference is the manner in which the members of the two societies approach problems. Americans, at least in the rational approach model, tend to make a series of analyses preliminary to a decision. The Vietnamese behave the opposite: they start with the goal and work backward—in effect deciding pragmatically what they want to achieve and then finding means to achieve it. This difference should not be overstressed, for we frequently do the same thing. In deciding how to go about it, however, they include such considerations as harmony and saving face, which are not usually elements in the American approach to problem-solving.

A fourth attitudinal difference is that toward leadership. For the Vietnamese leadership is personal, not institutional. It is the man who counts, at least as long as he holds power. Therefore, while the leader is expected to act in the general interest, he is permitted to do some things in his own interest. Thus a district chief who improves his fortunes in the process of building a new bridge is not criticized, provided that the bridge actually gets built.

Finally, a great importance is attached to the extended family and to village and ancestors. An American may view an official as corrupt if he helps his family with official funds, but a Vietnamese might consider him irresponsible for not doing so.

These varying attitudes in regard to tradition, harmony, approaching problems, leadership, and the family did not make the role of adviser easy for Americans with a "can do" ethos. In the course of advising the South Vietnamese, we did in fact meddle deeply in their polity, not always realizing the effect of such action.

Sometimes technically beneficial, our policy was in the aggregate counterproductive to the GVN in its attempt to convince the population that it was a sovereign state. For example, United States advisers prepared various plans for the ARVN, and sometimes directed the operation of ARVN units. As a result, many Vietnamese became convinced that the United States was in effect governing their country. Although some of these measures may have been necessary in the mid 1960's for the survival of the state, the eventual result was an inability of the GVN to demonstrate that it really represented the Vietnamese cause. In contrast, Ho Chi Minh and his followers from the early days were able to demonstrate a high degree of independence and concern for national interests. The outcome was that the GVN lacked political influence over the population, a disadvantage that continued throughout the long war.

Operationally, this lack of political influence and overidentification with a foreign power resulted in a phenomenon with which all advisers were familiar: insufficient motivation within the ARVN. Try as we might to stimulate it, it was never there. David Halberstam tells of a conversation with an army major, a defector from the North, during which Halberstam asked him what he could do if given an ARVN battalion to command. He responded: "I could command a division in North Vietnam. But a platoon here, even a squad, I could not do that. What can you do? They have no purpose."[2]

Another area with which the United States was never able to come to grips in its relationship with the South Vietnamese regime was the corruption endemic in the society. What was in the end self-defeating was the grossly outrageous nature of that corruption: the purchase of positions, the black market, the diversion of American assistance. It began near the top and worked its way down. The wife of the head of the Joint General Staff was reportedly deeply involved, even to the point of having officers transferred. The corps commanders were also reportedly involved, as were many division commanders. Province and district chiefs were in some cases so openly culpable that Americans documented the cases, but to no avail. Almost everyone was selling something.

2. David Halberstam, "Return to Vietnam," *Harper's Magazine* (December 1967), p. 52.

How could an army or a government so grossly corrupt, even in a country where corruption is expected, summon the enthusiastic support of its soldiers or its people? There was no way to do so, as successive American advisers discovered.

THE SOUTH VIETNAMESE LEADERSHIP

The South Vietnamese generals from President Thieu on down were younger than their American counterparts. They have been accused of being the worst officer corps in the world—plagued with corruption and politics.[3] Most of the generals entered the Army at about the age of twenty in the 1940's, some early in the next decade. Most started out in enlisted ranks and had a civilian educational level roughly equivalent to an American high school. Most could carry on a superficial conversation in English, and a substantial number could conduct conversations in depth. Most could express themselves with greater precision in French. Not many American generals could be classified as fluent in that language.

President Nguyen Van Thieu was born in 1923 in central Vietnam. During the Japanese occupation of World War II, he was involved in Ho Chi Minh's movement, but broke with it soon after the war. He was admitted to the first class at the Military School at Dalat, graduating as a warrant officer in 1949. By 1962 he was a colonel commanding the Fifth Infantry Division just north of Saigon. By virtue of this position, he was able to play an important role in the coup that overthrew Diem in 1963. For these services he received his first star and became part of the military junta. He eventually became the sole political survivor of this group, gaining command of the Fourth Corps in the Delta. Subsequently, he served as Minister of Defense and in 1965 became Chief of State when Ky was Premier. Under the new constitution in 1967 he was elected President, a position he retained until the final debacle in the spring of 1975. Since then, he has seemed to move between attractive homes in Taipei, London, and the south of France.

One of the older general officers was Nguyen Van Vy, born in 1916, who had joined the Army in 1936 and was in France in exile

3. John M. Mecklin, "An Alternative Strategy for Vietnam," *Fortune* (April 1968).

for seven or more years, returning after the 1963 coup against Diem. After the 1967 election of Thieu, Vy became Minister of Defense, a position he held during most of the remaining life of the republic. Vy himself had a reputation for integrity, honesty, and competence. He was never enchanted by Americans, but accepted them as a necessary evil.

Cao Van Vien, who was born in 1921, was one of the more unusual South Vietnamese generals. At the time of the coup against Diem, he commanded the airborne forces and refused to violate his oath and participate in the coup. For this he was briefly imprisoned and almost shot. Subsequently, he became commander of the III Corps (the eleven provinces around Saigon) and in late 1966 was named Chief Joint General Staff, a position he held throughout most of the remainder of the war. Vien became a qualified helicopter pilot in 1967. He refused to live on the guarded military compound with the other senior Saigon generals and retained the house in Saigon that he had owned since he was a major. He seemed to be without political ambition and led a spartan life— never drinking or smoking. Although his wife allegedly carried on many business activities, his involvement is not clear. He moved to northern Virginia after the government collapse and took up residence in an $80,000 house.

The commanders of the four corps in South Vietnam were among the most powerful men in the country during the period of the American military intervention. They varied in leadership qualities, capability, and corruptibility. One of the most colorful of the entire group was Do Cao Tri, who was born in 1929 in Bien Hoa and commissioned a lieutenant upon graduation from the Military Academy in 1947. He was in exile from 1964 until 1968, but during the last part of that absence served as Ambassador to Korea. Tri returned in mid-1968 to assume command of the Third Corps. He was an outstanding combat leader and was known to stand up in a tank to lead his men against the "communists," as he was fond of calling the enemy forces. Tri was independently wealthy, but there is some disagreement about the source of his money. He loved the good life, the best champagne and foods, and stories of his extracurricular activities abound. He was, however, one of the best leaders in South Vietnam until his untimely death in a helicopter accident near Tay Ninh City in 1971.

Below the Corps were the ten ARVN Infantry Divisions, whose

commanders had territorial responsibility for the part of the country to which they were assigned, essentially on a permanent basis. The capability of these commanders was a key factor in the performance of the South Vietnamese forces. Unlike the United States Army, the ARVN division commanders kept a tight control of all operations and activities, which unfortunately allowed little leeway for initiative on the part of subordinates.

There was great variation in the quality of these division commanders. Those who were corrupt and insisted on payoffs and bribes put severe pressure on their subordinates to do the same. Occasionally, United States representatives could get a corrupt division commander removed, but even then there was no certainty that the replacement would be an improvement.

United States senior advisers set down comments on the division commanders they worked with. In one such group of comments made in early 1970, of the ten men considered four were rated as very poor, one being described as a "coward and military incompetent"; two were rated as fair; three as good; and one as outstanding—"better than most United States division commanders." This last-named officer, who was consistently rated very high, was Ngo Quang Truong.

Truong, who had the misfortune of commanding the corps in the northern part of South Vietnam during the final debacle, was born in 1929 and entered the military around 1949. As a colonel, he was given command of the demoralized First Infantry Division in 1966. He served in that position for four years before taking command of the corps in the Delta. Under his command the First Division soon became the best in the Army. By a wide margin, he was considered the best combat commander in the South Vietnamese Army. After the final battles, when he commanded the First Corps in the North, he escaped by ship and, like Vien, resettled in northern Virginia.

At echelons below division, the war caused a considerable drain on qualified leadership. Many leaders were killed in combat or executed by the Viet Cong. Since many of them were political appointees, little incentive existed to exhibit initiative in lower ranks. Also, the manpower requirements for leadership at all levels went well beyond the supply of qualified persons. There was in addition a noticeable reluctance to open leadership training and positions to persons of lower social status.

In our questionnaire the American generals were asked how they would rate their Vietnamese counterparts:

ARVN general officer leadership as you viewed it when
you were in Vietnam was   *Percentage*
   (1) Quite strong   6
   (2) As good as could be expected—fair to good   57
   (3) Inadequate   32
   (4) Other or no answer   5

In the commentary many praised General Truong. Most comments concerned the problem of combining the political appointment of individuals in favor with Thieu with tactical and leadership competence. A premium was not always placed on the latter factors, and certainly political perceptions kept many of those identified as incompetent from being replaced.

ADVISING

Although this book is concerned with the 1965–72 period of United States intervention, the American advisory effort went back many years before that. The Geneva Accords developed in the summer of 1954 provided for the departure of the French military command, which was finally dissolved in April 1956. There was a period of almost two years after the Accords when both the United States and France had military headquarters in Saigon.

One provision of the Accords forbade any increase in external personnel, such as the United States Military Assistance Advisory Group (MAAG), which had been in South Vietnam assisting the French since 1950. As it happened, the size of the MAAG was 342 personnel when the Accords went into effect. In October of 1954 the MAAG Chief, Lieutenant General J. W. O'Daniel, was instructed to assist the South Vietnamese in "setting in motion a crash program designed to bring about an improvement in the loyalty and effectiveness of the Free Vietnamese forces."[4]

O'Daniel complained that he needed twice as many personnel to train the new forces and oversee the redistribution of United States equipment already in Vietnam as a result of United States support for the French prior to the Accords. In response to

4. *PP*, Vol. 2, pp. 432–434.

O'Daniel's request, a Temporary Equipment Recovery Team of 350 personnel was created. This combined force thus gave the MAAG Chief a staff of about 700, a figure that was maintained for the next seven years.

The United States MAAG gradually elbowed the remaining French out of the way. Its mission was to help the Vietnamese military to plan, recruit, organize, equip, and train the armed forces of South Vietnam. In those years the United States was also engaged in Korea in a massive advisory effort to assist in the development of the Korean armed forces. There was on the surface a remarkable similarity between the two situations: one country divided into two at an arbitrary parallel of latitude, one side of which was communist and the other noncommunist, with one side receiving United States support and the other receiving or at least having the possibility of Sino-Soviet support.

It is probably not surprising, then, that the work of the MAAG in Vietnam was modeled after what was happening in Korea. Although O'Daniel was charged with training the Vietnamese forces against both external attack and internal insurgency, the instructions were ambiguous. It was natural, therefore, for the MAAG to do what it knew best: place emphasis on a conventional force organized into battalions, regiments, and divisions. These units in turn were to be trained primarily in concepts of conventional warfare, the underlying premise of which was that such units would also be adequate for matters of internal security. When in 1959 and 1960 it became evident that the immediate threat was internal and not a matter of cross-border attack, it was probably too late to make any major changes in the Army of South Vietnam.

The more aggressive stance of the Kennedy Administration and the impact of the Taylor mission in the fall of 1961 have previously been mentioned. As in other areas, the advisory effort was affected. By the time of the Taylor mission in 1961, the VC had in fact gained the upper hand in the countryside. The increase in advisory effort beginning late in 1961 resulted from the Taylor mission. By December, the effort had doubled and by the following month more than tripled, reaching 3,400 personnel by April 1962. Still, this advisory effort did not send advisers below province level on the civil side, or regimental level on the military side.

The next benchmark in the advisory effort came in 1964 and was based upon two factors. It became evident in the aftermath of the coup against Diem that things were far worse for the Saigon government than had previously been realized. There had also developed with the increased effort since 1961 a strengthened conviction in Washington and Saigon that the struggle in Vietnam was so important to us that we could not afford to lose. The second factor was the arrival of a new COMUSMACV, General W. C. Westmoreland, who assumed that position in mid-1964. The result was an increase of 1,000 American advisers, to be placed for the first time at the battalion and districts levels,[5] the assumption being that greater United States presence would improve Vietnamese performance.

This was how things stood when bad defeats for ARVN forces in the spring and summer of 1965 made clear that if the country was to be held, United States troops would have to intervene. The advisory effort to date had failed and for a time it would have to be subordinated to the United States operational effort. It was always understood, however, that the advisory role would emerge as the key element at some later stage and its growth therefore continued during the period of United States operations. By October 1967 there were more than 10,000 United States military advisers in Vietnam, and by mid-1969, when United States strength in Vietnam peaked, there were 13,500 Army advisers alone.[6] In that peak year costs for the United States operational effort were $17.6 billion, and United States costs for South Vietnamese Armed Forces were $2.6 billion.

Staffing the advisory effort in Vietnam was an uphill battle from the outset. In the early stages the effort was slowed by difficulties in adviser selection and training, a general lack of adviser motivation, and a failure to appreciate the problems related to advising societies with an alien culture. The last point had to be kept in mind at all levels, as illustrated by a memorandum to Ambassador Bunker from General Lansdale a few days before the Tet 1968 offensive:

> At Tet with the advent of the new year, it would be useful to keep in mind that certain of the dates in the year ahead will be

5. A district was a subgovernmental agency to the 44 provinces in South Vietnam. There were in all approximately 250 districts (their boundaries were adjusted from time to time), and the increased advisory effort was designed to place advisory teams in about half of them.

6. Of these advisers, 6,500 were in the pacification effort discussed later in this chapter.

looked upon by most Vietnamese as inauspicious days. The dates are given below for the guidance of those who wonder at the Vietnamese reluctance to undertake new projects on such days:

February 3, 12, 21	August 7, 16, 28
March 3, 12, 21	September 6, 15, 26
April 2, 11, 20	October 5, 14, 23
May 1, 10, 19, 31	November 4, 13, 24
June 9, 19, 30	December 3, 12, 24
July 9, 18, 29	

A more important cultural difference was Vietnamese sensitivity about saving face. This was especially the case in the advisory effort, where care had to be taken that Vietnamese commanders did not feel subordinate to an American adviser or headquarters. Results were mixed. One of the most successful of all advisers, although not always approved of by higher American headquarters, was John Paul Vann. Vann early in the war was an Army officer working as an adviser in the upper Delta. Personally courageous, blunt, and bright, he deserves a full-scale biography. He understood the situation clearly and reported it the way it was—a proclivity that did not endear him to the optimistic General Paul Harkins, Westmoreland's predecessor.[7] Despite Vann's rapport with his Vietnamese counterparts, he could rarely get them to emulate his courage and commitment. After all, their motivation to rise to their position in the first place had been to separate themselves from the rank and file and all attendant miseries. The notion of leadership for the South Vietnamese was of a different cultural dimension from the American.

An example that focuses the advisory problem even more clearly is the Chinh-Hunnicutt case. In late 1966 General Phan Truong Chinh was commander of the south Vietnamese 25th Infantry Division, considered at that time the least effective of all ARVN divisions. Whatever his motive, the division commander had reached the point where he was no longer conducting military operations; he was in fact interfering with those who were trying to

7. Vann, after falling into disfavor with Harkins, returned to the United States and subsequently left the service. He later returned to Vietnam as a high-ranking civilian and served in various locations until he was killed in action late in the war as senior adviser in the II Corps area.

conduct operations in his area. His senior adviser was an aggressive and competent American infantry colonel, Cecil Hunnicutt.

Chinh's actions caused Hunnicutt to send a confidential report on him to Westmoreland. Naturally, Chinh obtained a copy of the report. In retaliation, Chinh issued an order of the day which forbade his officers from having anything to do with their advisers. After high-level intervention, the order was rescinded. Hunnicutt completed his tour and received the Legion of Merit upon departure. The affair illustrated, however, how impossible it was to breach the culture gap sufficiently to elicit adequate performance from ARVN through the advisory system. On the surface, the Chinh case was extreme, but only on the surface. The advisory system never really worked.

Many observers were critical of Westmoreland in this regard, stating that he had abdicated his responsibilities toward the Vietnamese.[8] In effect, the charge was that because he was unable to get them to produce, he ignored them, accepting at face value what they said they were doing. This raises the question of the leverage the Americans were able to bring to bear on the Vietnamese, a matter we will come to shortly. First, it will be useful to quote what some of the American Army generals had to say about the advisory effort:

> There were too many advisers. The result was, advisers became operators and diverted the energy of their ARVN counterparts from their primary mission and at the same time left little incentive for the ARVN commanders to take actions of their own.

> Any single Vietnamese commander was exposed to from 8 to 28 different American advisers over the years. There was a lack of continuity and many divergent approaches to the same problem. This led to a lack of initiative and foot-dragging on the part of ARVN.

> On my first trip to Vietnam, I made a visit to a Vietnamese battalion near the Laotian border. The Battalion Commander had commanded the battalion for six years. His adviser was an

---

8. Halberstam, p. 50. Westmoreland felt that he did exercise adequate leverage on the Vietnamese. See *A Soldier Reports*, p. 240.

American Second Lieutenant. He was not really an adviser,
only a liaison officer for U.S. resources.

If I were a Vietnamese, I would have been overwhelmed by
the Americans, if not in numbers, then in energy, ideas and
activity. This is not the Vietnamese way of doing things. We
focused on everything to the point where the Vietnamese had
no idea of priority.

We erroneously tried to impose the American system on a
people who didn't want it, couldn't handle it and may lose
because they tried it.

In this, as in all our foreign wars, we never really established
rapport. This was largely due to our overinflated hypnosis
with the myth that the American way—in economics, politics,
sociology, manners, morals, military equipment, methodol-
ogy, organization, tactics, etc—is automatically and unchal-
lengeably the best (really the only) way to do things. This failing may well be the area of greatest weakness for the future of
American arms.

We never took into account the cultural differences. We tried
to use the advisory methods of Korea in Vietnam. They were
not applicable. The Koreans perceived they were struggling
to survive. The Vietnamese perceived it differently—their
environment was more benevolent in their eyes.

We were really quite indifferent to the improvement of
ARVN. Most of us did not want to associate with them.

Given the scope of the United States advisory effort and the
problems of interaction with the Vietnamese, how successful were
we in bringing leverage to bear on the Vietnamese leadership? The
answer is, not very successful. General Taylor's recommendations
of 1961, which led to a step-up of the advisory effort, emphasized a
close working relationship as a means of improving Vietnamese
forces. To go further, any type of United States command would
have been an encroachment on Vietnamese sovereignty, and it was
perceived that this would have been counterproductive to GVN
development even if the Vietnamese had permitted it, which they
would not. Hence, some means of persuasion had to be developed
to secure improvements, and this was the central problem of the
advisory effort for its remaining eleven years. Westmoreland opted

for various coordinating devices to help upgrade Vietnamese forces, but his early suggestion for a combined American-Vietnamese coordinating staff was resisted by Thieu and others, and was dropped. Thereafter, he leaned heavily on persuasion and example, although leverage remained an issue throughout the war. Defense Secretary McNamara was a consistent advocate of increased and direct leverage to secure better results from the GVN leadership. In this, he never prevailed. There were also those in the field who from time to time suggested withdrawing support and advice from certain very deficient ARVN units. Westmoreland would almost never permit this.

Two studies in Washington specifically addressed the question of leverage. The first was an Army staff study called PROVN, done at the request of Army Chief of Staff General Harold K. Johnson in 1965 and 1966. It proposed that leverage be employed at all levels within the GVN on a "continuum from subtle interpersonal persuasion to withdrawal of American support."[9] The study received wide distribution in Washington and elsewhere, and comments were solicited from COMUSMACV. In reply, Westmoreland dissented, responding that there were substantial difficulties and dangers in implementing such a program. The other study, completed in the summer of 1967 in a small office in the White House, was concerned with pacification and forwarded by the State Department to Saigon. The reply, which came from Ambassador Robert Komer, Westmoreland's Deputy for pacification, in effect rejected the study's proposal for using increased leverage. However, Komer's operation, as we will see subsequently, did successfully develop a type of leverage against incompetent officials.

Two events did increase United States leverage on the Vietnamese to improve their performance. The first was in the aftermath of Tet 68, when the GVN needed all the support from the United States that it could get, both material and psychological. The other was the announcement in 1969 by the Nixon Administration of the Vietnamization program. When it became evident to the GVN that within a few years they would be on their own, United States suggestions for improvement were more closely listened to.[10]

9. *PP*, Vol. 2, p. 501.

10. An interesting and authoritative discussion of leverage and related matters is in Lawrence E. Grinter, "Bargaining Between Saigon and Washington: Dilemmas of Linkage Politics During War," *Orbis*, 18 (1974), 837–867.

I asked a former Deputy COMUSMACV how much leverage he felt we had. His response was very little except on an interpersonal basis in particular cases. Another senior officer who had long experience as an adviser responded to a similar question as follows: "We were captured by the Vietnamese. We never did lay it on the line to them. We were in the hands of a French-trained bureaucracy whom we never controlled, nor did we ever get their priorities straightened out."

The present survey did not contain any question on this issue, but the answer to a 1966 Army survey of 330 officer advisers and former advisers is revealing:[11]

What was the best technique for bringing pressure on the Vietnamese to perform better?	Percentage
(1) By establishing a close personal relationship with my counterpart	56
(2) By withdrawal of military resources	12
(3) By control of funds	11
(4) By bringing pressure to bear through the next higher U.S.-GVN echelon	21

THE ARMY OF SOUTH VIETNAM

One of the topics most frequently discussed by the media throughout the long war was the quality of the Army of Vietnam, or ARVN.[12] The official line was that it was constantly improving, but representatives of the news media who were roaming the countryside were skeptical. There was good reason for skepticism, because serious problems existed—some of our own making, but many systemic. (The ARVN prior to Vietnamization is discussed at this point. That final attempt at improvement will be considered in Chapter 6.)

The first set of general problems besetting the ARVN were those

11. U.S. Department of Army, *Program for the Pacification and Long Term Development of South Vietnam* (PROVN), Vol. 2 (March 1966), p. G–37.

12. The United States had Air Force and Naval advisory efforts, but they were not of concern to most Army generals. Of concern, however, in addition to ARVN, were the Regional Forces and Popular Forces, discussed below.

concerned with organizational and operational issues. It is true that we built an army on what is sometimes called the Fort Benning model. It was organized into battalions, regiments, and divisions, large and powerful units designed for offensive action against enemy units. The force was heavily dependent on tank and artillery support and sophisticated air cover. All of this support was available, of course, as long as the American expeditionary force was around. The high-ranking generals who commanded these divisions were reluctant to break them down into small units for purposes of local security, even though frequently that was what the war was all about. Many had reasons to feel that the ARVN should have, in part at least, been organized differently. Its size, structure, and need for heavy-fire support made it an expensive army, for which the United States paid all the fighting costs and helped to pay the salaries of its soldiers. It was evident that the South Vietnamese economy alone could never support such a force. It probably should have been evident also that the United States public would not support such a force indefinitely.

There were other problems created by the way the army was organized. Firepower as employed by the ARVN, emulating United States methods, is highly destructive and frequently counterproductive in a counterinsurgency environment.[13] Additionally, the local security problem that we have already touched upon probably would have been better served by an army, in part at least, lightly armed and broken up in smaller formations, less dependent on sophisticated and expensive heavy-fire support.

Leaving aside what many perceived to be an organizational failure, how well did the Army do operationally? The overall answer is, sometimes quite well but often poorly. Some of the shortcomings were overdependence on heavy-fire support, unwillingness to fight at night or over long periods of time, lack of aggressiveness, and poor coordination. This last weakness was especially noticeable between the ARVN and the Vietnamese Air Force, which did not always accept mission requirements from the Army and frequently was unable or unwilling to accept changes in mission when the tactical situation required. Some of the

13. This was only one of many reasons why ARVN had poor relations with the population it was defending. In addition to being victimized by firepower and sometimes looting, the population had little reason to be confident in ARVN's ability to afford them lasting security—a fatal flaw in a counterinsurgency environment.

shortcomings were matters of morale and leadership which first manifested themselves as training problems. It should be added that when the Tet 1968 offensive came, the ARVN conducted itself quite well. Although undermanned because of holiday leaves, most units defended their positions satisfactorily and subsequently launched counterattacks. The official judgment was that, of the 149 ARVN infantry battalions, 42 performed exceptionally well and only 8 unsatisfactorily. There were no large-scale defections, and much more resolute combat than some had expected. We must not forget, however, that in early 1968 there was enormous United States presence and support.

Over the years from 1954 onward the United States advisory effort involved large-scale training. Since this effort was exerted simultaneously with the expansion of Vietnamese forces from something over 100,000 to over a million, many problems arose. None were more significant than the leadership shortage. Management of the 33 training centers was supervised by the Vietnamese Central Training Command, which was responsible for training at the national level. This was a very passive headquarters with little experience at supervising training on the scale required. The most significant obstacle to effective training, however, was poor leadership at the training center level. Frequently, the training posts were filled by officers who had been relieved of combat commands for being ineffective—a natural tendency, but over time damaging to the training effort. The war had dragged on so long that training became a business-as-usual affair, five days a week, eight hours a day. As a result, training for night fighting, at which the VC excelled, was nonexistent in the middle of this war for survival.

In addition to individual replacement training, there was, on paper at least, a unit training program. Commanders were supposed to conduct this training between combat operations. For the most part, however, the time was generally used for "rest and recuperation." There was also a refresher training program, in which ARVN units were rotated through training centers every two or three years. It was ineffective, owing to lack of interest, with some exceptions—the most notable being the excellent refresher training provided by the Australian Task Force in Phuoc Tuy Province.

There was also an elaborate military school system which at its peak totaled twenty-five schools. Two are worth noticing. The first was the Vietnamese National Military Academy, which in 1967 was converted from a two-year to a four-year school. Since this was Viet Nam's West Point, one might think graduates would emerge motivated to begin their careers as small-unit leaders. Not so. In one class around 1966, every infantry officer graduate expressed preference for duty in a division headquarters rather than in an infantry company. Second, in August 1967, in "recognition of the need to provide training to top military officers and government civilians for functions of national security," a National Defense College was established in Saigon. A perusal of the guide to study published by the College might make one think he was sitting back at the United States National War College in Washington. Topics such as "Making a National Strategic Appraisal" or "Selecting National Objectives and Courses of Action" may be suitable for contemplation when one represents a major world power. In the middle of a war for survival in a small Asian nation, however, the program seems out of place.

Several times I have alluded to the fact that the central problem of the ARVN was inadequate leadership. Poor leadership, including preoccupation with political maneuvering at the senior level and lack of experience at the junior officer level, were major difficulties. Junior officers were recruited and promoted more on the basis of family and economic status than of ability. There was never any systematic program to recruit or identify potentially good leadership from the ranks. There was too much emphasis on formal education as the primary criterion for becoming an officer, and not enough on other traits which would have provided a broader-based officer corps. As one general put it, there was a super-developed class sense inherited from the French. At the senior level, many of the Vietnamese generals didn't feel that anyone junior to them knew anything.

In the advisory context, the United States paid too little attention to the problem of military leadership. One perceptive observer, Robert Komer, has said:

Perhaps the greatest flaw was the failure to come to grips directly with the gross inadequacies of GVN and RVNAF leadership at all levels. U.S. advisers early recognized that this was the critical problem. But we usually drew the line at direct intervention. Instead of pressing for removal of unsatisfactory commanders, and if necessary suspending aid as a lever to this end, MACV and U.S. civilian agencies confined themselves to such indirect means as improved personnel selection procedures, schooling, and the like. These did not suffice; no matter how well trained, equipped, and organized the GVN and RVNAF became, poor leaders all too often remained its Achilles heel.[14]

As for the individual enlisted man of ARVN, many American generals felt he was a courageous fighter who, when well led, as in Truong's 1st Division, could match the VC or North Vietnamese soldier. However, morale, as indicated by high desertion rates, was not good. There were many reasons for this in addition to poor leadership. A survey conducted of ARVN enlisted men in 1970 revealed the following reasons for desertion in declining order of importance: first, family hardships and homesickness; second, inadequate living conditions; third, low pay; fourth, too many operations; and finally, fear of danger or death.[15]

Like all other aspects of the war, MACV headquarters managed to quantify estimates of effectiveness of South Vietnamese forces. For many years this was called the Senior Advisors Monthly Evaluation (SAME). The report was at first wholly narrative, but as the advisory mission grew, it became highly structured and quantified. Since more senior advisers were able to see the report of juniors, there was manipulation of the data both directly and indirectly. As in United States units, the senior officers in many cases felt their performance would be judged by such reports and were frequently anxious to give the impression of better results from their ARVN units than in fact were being achieved.

To overcome this and related problems, a new report was introduced toward the end of 1967 that consisted of 145 multiple-choice

14. *Bureaucracy Does Its Thing*, p. 124.

15. Actually, Vietnamese deaths from hostile action ran fairly high compared with the American. Obviously this would be the case beginning in 1970, as United States troops were being withdrawn. However, even during the period of major United States involvement it was true, as shown by the following figures of average monthly deaths.

Year	U.S.	RVNAF
1965	114	937
1966	417	996
1967	782	1060
1968	1216	2027
1969	785	1578
1970	352	1782

questions, which overcame at least direct manipulation of the data. Data were grouped into four categories and became the basis of comparative evaluation of all ARVN units. The categories were operational results in terms of kill ratio, etc.; combat strength in the field; estimates of combat strength of opposing enemy units; and estimates by advisers of ARVN leadership, training, and aggressiveness.

At the end of the survey administered to the Army general officers, there was a shopping list of matters on which, if they had it to do over again, they would recommend the greatest changes. Of the eight areas listed, the highest percentage received in any area (91) was for "Improving the ARVN."

The Pacification Effort[16]

Pacification in South Vietnam, sometimes called "winning the hearts and minds," denoted a combination of programs designed to extend, especially into rural areas, the presence and influence of the central government. Simultaneously, the goal was to reduce the influence and control of the Vietcong. Emphasis varied at different times and places, but in general there were two major elements to pacification. The first was provision of physical security to the population by neutralizing the Vietcong apparatus. The second was positive development programs designed to increase the support of the population for the central government.

During the postwar French period there were some local attempts at pacification programs but very little planning on the national level. The French were primarily concerned up until 1954 with military requirements for defeating the insurgency. The immediate preoccupation for Diem and the South Vietnamese leadership after the Geneva Accords was to care for the approximately 1,000,000 refugees coming from the North. Thereafter there began

16. An excellent perspective, to which I am indebted for several ideas in this portion of the book, is in Chester L. Cooper, et al., *The American Experience with Pacification in Vietnam*, Vol. 1, *An Overview of Pacification* (Arlington, Va., Institute for Defense Analysis, 1972). Volumes 2 and 3 apparently cover the matter in greater detail but remain classified at this writing.

a series of pacification plans called by various names: Civic Action (1955–56); Land Development Centers (1957–59); Agrovilles (1959–61); Strategic Hamlets (1961–63); Hop Tac, Chien Thang, and the New Life Hamlets (1964–65). For a variety of reasons, all of these efforts failed.[17]

By the time of the United States military intervention in 1965, pacification was being called "rural reconstruction." That year the situation of the central government continued to be shaky, with most efforts and resources going into combat activities. In 1966, thanks to United States intervention, the situation stabilized and a new pacification program, called "revolutionary development" got under way. True United States pacification began about that time, sparked by the Honolulu conference in February 1966. President Johnson, who called the conference, met with Generals Thieu and Ky, by now leaders of South Vietnam.

It was at this conference that LBJ insisted we could not fight just a military war but also had to fight the "other war." Robert Komer was appointed by the President to head pacification efforts from the White House, and subsequently an Office of Civil Operations was established in Saigon under Deputy Ambassador William Porter. The Embassy office proved inadequate, being dwarfed by the huge United States military effort then under way. The solution in 1967 was to place the United States pacification effort under General Westmoreland and give him Robert Komer as a civilian deputy. The new office, which combined Embassy and MACV efforts, was called Civil Operation and Revolutionary Development Support (CORDS) and became the instrument for the major United States pacification effort during the Vietnam War.

SECURITY AND DEVELOPMENT

From the outset of United States involvement it was recognized that the first essential of pacification was security for the rural population—to clear and hold local areas, to put it in military terms. The debate was about how it was to be provided. In the earlier stages the military viewed anything connected with pacification, including security, as a civilian problem. By 1966 this attitude

17. For a brief but very perceptive description of these efforts, see Lawrence E. Grinter, "Counter Insurgency," *Spectrum*, 3 (1975), 49–78.

had begun to change, and the fifty-nine man Revolutionary Development Teams provided a partial answer to the problem. Up to 1967, about half of the ARVN combat battalions were also assigned the security task, on a temporary basis.

But the answer to large-scale security required a permanent force engaged in that task alone. The solution decided on was to emphasize the Regional Forces and Popular Forces. Beginning about 1967, considerable effort was put into upgrading those forces, who were all locally recruited and in many cases were made up of volunteers who had sought to avoid being drafted into the regular forces.

Regional Force rifle companies operated either separately or in battalion formations. Their mission was to operate against Vietcong local forces within their own province. The objective was to attack the enemy as far as possible from the province's population centers and to serve as reaction forces. Popular Force platoons were intended to provide security for hamlets or villages against small numbers of VC guerrillas. The Popular Force soldier was recruited locally and stayed in his home village, where he participated in daylight security activities and night-time ambushes.

Between the mid-1960's and the early 1970's, the Regional and Popular Forces expanded from a combined force of about 150,000 to over 500,000. Another program involved security to some extent, although probably it was more important as a means of acquiring political commitment to the central government. This was the People's Self-Defense Force. This program had begun in 1963 but had been dormant for many years. The shock of Tet 1968 led to its revival. It was a part-time activity and at its peak reportedly had some four million members, of whom only a relatively small percentage were actually armed.

Although all of these forces were of assistance in denying the insurgents access to the population and establishing some degree of law and order, one important security pacification objective was being ignored—neutralizing the clandestine VC political-administrative apparatus, usually called the VC infrastructure (VCI). This was the secret government which levied taxes, controlled its own local insurgent forces, recruited replacements, and administered the areas it controlled. In addition, the VCI supported military operations of the Vietcong and North Vietnamese Army main force units by providing intelligence, recruits, and logistic support. Their tools were propaganda and terror, and to combat them or root them out the GVN instituted a program of its own, which involved terror tactics: the Phung Hoang or Phoenix Program. It stemmed from a GVN Presidential decree of July 1968 and included an intelligence program to identify members of the VCI, an operational program to apprehend them, and a "legal" program to confine them. The program operated at each level of administration—national, provincial, district, and village. Dossiers were developed on suspects, but the information in them was, in many cases, considered highly unreliable. From its inception in 1968 until United States participation was closed out in late 1972, the United States supported the Program with almost four million dollars. In addition, United States advisers participated in the Program, with a peak strength of about 700 being reached in 1970. During the course of the Program, over 81,000 VC were "neutralized." Of this total, over 26,000 were killed and the remaining either came in on their own and were released, or were captured and detained.

Most of the VC who were tried appeared before an informal judicial security committee (An Tri), which could sentence a suspect to up to two years in jail. Many allegations were made concerning the Program: torture, assassination, innocent people jailed through false testimony, etc. We may not know the full story of the Phung Hoang Program for some years, if ever. However, there was considerable criticism, probably justified, of United States funding and advisory participation. Some allege that such activities conflict with standard American precepts and are in fact criminal and a violation of the Hague Regulations on warfare.[18] In any case, it seems clear that the entire issue will have to be reexamined in the future, before United States personnel become involved again in an internal security operation of this nature.

Let us turn now to the other half of the pacification effort—development of civil programs. Before the establishment of a single United States manager for pacification, a variety of different agencies existed, all with their own pipelines to Washington. One of these, the United States Agency for International Development (AID), was mainly concerned with civil development. In the early period this was largely confined to refugee relief and projects such as road building.

18. For discussion of both sides of this issue by Richard Falk, a professor at Princeton, and Robert Komer, see Trooboff, *Law and Responsibility in Warfare*.

Refugees in Vietnam were frequently featured in stories in United States newspapers—in part, because of the efforts of Senator Edward Kennedy, who was very concerned about the problem. They remained a problem throughout most of the war, even contributing to the rout of the South Vietnamese Army in 1975 by clogging the roads. The refugee problem was caused in part by the people's desire to flee the war itself. In addition, however, it represented a conscious decision to relocate certain persons out of VC areas whether they wanted to be relocated or not. A good deal of the resources in the pacification effort were directed toward trying to solve the human problems involved.

By the early 1960's the development effort had begun to focus on the rural population in an attempt to improve their standard of living. However, there was a divergency of opinion on priorities among those who favored the traditional approach of long-term development of the government's economic institutions and those who wanted immediate benefits for the people. The latter group argued that time was of the essence, and that it was important for the Saigon government to get the people's loyalty lest there be no long-term economic institutions. The divergence arose again when CORDS became the single manager of pacification in 1967. The outcome was that efforts were divided between both kinds of programs.

The CORDS Program, beginning in 1967, placed development emphasis in three areas inherited from AID. The first was revival of the rural administration at the village and hamlet level, which had been abolished by Diem in the mid-1950's. Second, there was an attempt to revive the depressed economics of the rural areas through agricultural improvements and upgrading roads and waterways. Third, an effort was made to improve rural services in such areas as medical care and education.

Understandably, all of these attempts at development, since they were occurring simultaneously, placed a considerable strain on the Vietnamese ability to implement them and had undesirable side effects. Some local corruption was unavoidable, considering the lavish nature of the aid. There was also engendered an unhealthy dependence on the United States for programs which most rural Vietnamese would normally consider luxuries and many of which they could not continue after United States departure.

General Moshe Dayan described the problem after a tour of South Vietnam in the spring of 1968. He claimed that too much was being done for local Vietnamese Administration. As a result, the would-be Vietnamese administrators were being discouraged, and the population at large was not involved, thus giving VN of ficials an excuse for their own lack of enthusiasm and participation. Foreign troops, he said, never win the hearts of the people.

ORGANIZING FOR PACIFICATION

To head the new pacification effort, Robert Komer, as previously mentioned, was appointed Westmoreland's Deputy. He was already well known in Vietnam because of his frequent trips from Washington on behalf of the White House. He projected an image of arrogance and of great power with the President. It was said that he had more signed photographs of LBJ in his Saigon office than any other United States official in Vietnam.

Komer spent about fifteen years with the CIA before becoming a member of the National Security Council Staff and thus taking on the White House pacification job. Articulate, brash, bright, and abrasive, he left many bruised egos behind. Stories about him in his Saigon days abound. As Deputy to Westmoreland, he had the assumed rank of a four-star general. One day a military policeman failed to recognize him and held up his car to let that of a Brigadier General go by. Komer immediately insisted on plates with four stars and received something equivalent, which he occasionally used. Komer's ability to communicate directly with the President could have created problems for Westmoreland. On one occasion, at the President's request, Komer wrote LBJ a comparative appraisal of Generals Westmoreland and Abrams. Westmoreland came out best. Early in his stay Komer sent several "back channel" messages to the White House without clearance with either COMUSMACV or the Ambassador. In one instance he suggested that the President send his message back as a directive to Westmoreland and Bunker. What Komer did not know was that both the Commanding General and the Ambassador were automatically on distribution for these "private" messages.

Notwithstanding these aspects of his personality, Robert Komer was one of the most competent and effective high-level American officials to serve in Vietnam. He was by nature the hard-driving type, living up to the name given him by Ambassador Lodge, "Blowtorch." He accepted the political assumptions behind the

United States pacification programs and bent his efforts toward making them work. His first contribution was to tie together the diverse programs by setting up CORDS as a more effective organization than anything that had preceded it.

The CORDS organization was unique. It was not independent but an administrative service which operated with the resources and personnel of several agencies, including the Department of Defense and AID. At its Saigon headquarters it had eleven directorates, which in addition to performing its own administrative functions advised its counterparts in the Government of Vietnam's ministries. CORDS field personnel came under the direct control of Komer.

CORDS personnel came from all the military services, the State Department, from AID, CIA, and the United States Information Service. There were four regional deputies for CORDS, civilians who theoretically served under the United States senior officer in each of the four Corps Tactical Zones in Vietnam and advised each of the Vietnamese Corps.[19] In each zone there were also CORDS advisory teams in each province and district. About half the provincial senior advisers were civilians, and at district level almost all advisers were military personnel. Below the corps level, the new organization removed both United States and GVN military organizations from the formal chain of command.

The organization seemed to work, although there were complaints. One senior general felt that the senior United States military in each Corps Zone, such as the Field Force Commanders, were pacification bosses in name only. In effect they were required to go along with whatever the CORDS chain of command decided. Some United States division commanders complained of problems of coordination with CORDS on a day-to-day basis. Also, some CORDS advisers at province and district level felt their power was very limited, since AID personnel seemed to have more influence in terms of controlling resources.

In CORDS, as in the military advisory system, a big issue was leverage with Vietnamese counterparts. In the CORDS context the targets of leverage were five: (1) creating a GVN governmental structure that was responsive to requirements of the people; (2)

19. John Paul Vann was the first appointed to and served initially in the III Corps Tactical Zone, which comprised the eleven provinces around Saigon.

raising the quality of the GVN leadership; (3) stimulating an effective GVN performance; (4) encouraging greater integrity on the part of South Vietnamese officials; and (5) protecting United States interests where our allies appeared to be taking advantage of us. Komer made a determined effort to exert leverage on the Vietnamese and was in fact probably more successful in the area of dealing with corrupt officials than any other part of the American establishment in Vietnam. In January 1968 he issued a policy statement to his corps advisers in which he emphasized that leverage should be applied in a series of graduated steps, with the more drastic actions reserved to his office because of the potentially explosive nature of pressuring GVN officials. The government of Vietnam was, after all, a sovereign nation.

Komer's plan entailed verbal discussion by senior CORDS officials in the field with unresponsive GVN officials, followed by letters if necessary, and the building up of a dossier, which as a final step would be forwarded to CORDS in Saigon. The problem was a difficult one, however, and the threat of withdrawing aid to a particular area was ineffective, since the GVN was aware that the United States had as much to lose from withdrawal as did they. It was a frustrating situation for CORDS officials. The best course seemed to be the relief of selected officials, especially where corruption could be proven. In this Komer and those who followed him were fairly successful. Komer managed to have about half the province chiefs removed, and over one quarter of the district chiefs. The problem was how to replace them with someone better. In this there was considerably less success.

The generals who participated in the survey were asked one question concerning the CORDS record:

Administration (of the pacification program):	*Percentage*
(1) Should have been completely administered by United States military	17
(2) The CORDS arrangement under a military field force commander or equivalent was the optimum arrangement	26
(3) More should have been done by the Vietnamese	44
(4) Other or no answer	13

There was little commentary on this question by respondents. The response to item 4 was large because about 10 percent of the respondents selected both items 2 and 3, and I coded such cases as "other." In effect, then, 36 percent approved the CORDS arrangement, but 54 percent felt more should have been done by the Vietnamese.

MEASURING RESULTS

In the previous chapter we considered the problems associated with measuring progress in the main-force war. Efforts to measure progress or results in pacification got under way much later and took a somewhat different twist. In the early days of the advisory effort, no one, except perhaps the CIA, paid much attention to reporting on what was happening in the countryside in Vietnam. McNamara's arrival on the Washington scene in 1961 spurred interest in statistical reports in general and eventually in pacification efforts and results in Vietnam. This in turn generated efforts in Saigon to coordinate the reports of the various elements in the American mission. However, reliance was almost wholly based on Vietnamese sources and the subjective judgments of United States advisers.

By 1966 pacification had come to be of great interest in Washington; McNamara and CIA Director Helms agreed that something had to be done about pacification reporting. The result was the institution of the Hamlet Evaluation System (HES) in January 1967.[20] Given the scope of the problem—44 provinces, approximately 250 districts, 2,300 villages, and 13,000 hamlets—any reporting system obviously had to be designed for input from relatively unskilled field advisers.

Basically, each district adviser was asked to select a response from a series of indicators that best described the conditions in each village and hamlet in his area. Indicators were in two groups of nine each; one group described the security condition in the area and the other described development programs. All of the reports were computerized, and after tabulation and analysis they became the basis for monthly pacification reports from Saigon to Washington and for Saigon's estimate of progress, or lack of it, in the countryside. In effect, it was a detailed gazetteer of the situation in the Vietnam countryside.

20. There were numerous other subsidiary systems which reported on specific programs related to pacification, but HES was the most important and best known.

This reporting system had many faults, but it was a start. In 1970 an improved system was installed which was much more objective and sophisticated than its predecessor. It restricted advisers largely to responding to a series of objective questions. Subsequent changes may have overdone this approach. The system became a highly sophisticated and uniquely American enterprise which depended on a large advisory presence throughout the country. It had its critics, but the Army general officers gave it fairly good marks compared with their negative reaction to the system that reported on the main-force war.

The hamlet evaluation system (as modified) was   *Percentage*
   (1) A good way to measure progress in pacification   2
   (2) Had weaknesses but was about as good as could be
       devised   75
   (3) Not a valid way to measure progress in pacification   19
   (4) No answer   4

Some in the Embassy were more critical than the generals were, judging by the above figures. One official there in early 1970 told me that the gaps between HES numbers and actual conditions in the provinces had reached ludicrous proportions. He pointed out that although the report showed that the III Corps area, which I was in, contained five provinces controlled 100 percent by the central government, there were three in which neither of us could drive safely if unescorted. He was right.

One example will suffice to show how selected reporters (i.e., not the everyday, working in Vietnam reporter) and high-ranking officials could be misled on this matter. The December 29, 1969, issue of *Newsweek* carried an article by the late Stewart Alsop, in which he described an unescorted automobile tour with Ambassador William Colby, Komer's successor at CORDS, from Ca Mau to Can Tho in the Delta. Alsop waxed enthusiastic about this trip as an example of the impressive gains in pacification. What actually happened—unknown to Alsop and, I assume, Colby—was that they in fact had a large military escort. United States armed teams preceded and followed the car, close enough to provide protection but distant enough not to be seen by occupants. A number of armed helicopters, out of sight, also accompanied the "unescorted" tour, and outposts along the way were constantly informed of their progress. Unfortunately, this kind of deception was not uncommon.

 # People Problems

Professionalism

In April 1970, General Westmoreland, then Chief of Staff of the Army, wrote a letter to the Commandant of the Army War College asking for a study of the "Moral and Professional Climate in the Army." The occasion for the letter, said Westmoreland, was "several unfavorable events occurring within the Army during the past few years." "Several unfavorable events" was something of an understatement. There had been war crimes at My Lai and elsewhere, including alleged cover-ups by senior officers. There were corruption cases involving, among others, the former Provost Marshal of the Army; a general in charge of administration and services at the Army Headquarters in Long Binh; and the former Sergeant Major of the Army while he had been serving in Vietnam. There were also many allegations of careerism—medals for senior officers, perhaps not always deserved, and body count fabrications.

In any case, the professionalism Westmoreland was referring to involved a combination of ethics, professional competence, and performance. The study, finished in a very short time, did indeed find that there was a "significant difference between ideal values of the officer corps and its operative values." The pressures causing this gap, the report stated, stemmed from a combination of self-oriented, success-motivated actions and a lack of professional skills on the part of middle and senior grade officers. Particularly singled out was the importance of short-term statistical indicators of success for those who were having their chance at command.

Much has now been done to clear up these problems, but the report serves as a good indication of professional attitudes during the war in Vietnam, not all of which had their origin there. I included several questions on professionalism in my survey. Reading over the answers, I note that the questions appeared to equate professionalism, at least by suggestion, with competence, and by implication excluded considerations of careerism which relate to ethical issues. That will become clear as we examine the response to a question regarding careerism. The following, therefore, should be viewed as inquiring about competence:[1]

Professionalism of U.S. Army Officer Corps in
Vietnam:

		Percentage	
		Lower Ranks	*Middle Ranks*
(1)	Highly professional	62	70
(2)	Fairly professional	31	26
(3)	Left a good deal to be desired	6	2
(4)	No answer	1	2

Compared to the Korean War or World War II,
United States army officers in Vietnam were:

		Percentage	
		WW II	*Korean War*
(1)	More professional	43	33
(2)	About the same	35	47
(3)	Less professional	12	10
(4)	No answer	10	10

Subsequently, however, a question on careerism elicited a different kind of response, which will serve as a basis for further discussion of that issue.

Careerism (i.e. ticket punching, rapid rotation in
jobs, etc.) was:

	Percentage
(1) No problem	9
(2) Somewhat of a problem	50
(3) A serious problem	37
(4) No answer	4

During the advisory days of the Army's involvement in Vietnam, career "security" lay in an advisory job with a Vietnamese troop unit. This was especially true for the job of Division Adviser. After

1. A separate question asked the generals to identify the greatest strength of the officer corps in Vietnam. In response, 59 percent named leadership ability; 24 percent, technical competence; and 7 percent, tactical ability. The remainder either did not answer or combined some questions.

the United States troop intervention, the situation changed, and a combat command at battalion level for lieutenant colonels and at brigade level for colonels became the essential requirement. Great emphasis has always been placed on the command requirement for combat arms officers looking for stars, or, indeed, even for promotion. Command in combat was even more important than peacetime command. Not only was it necessary to command, but it was necessary to get an "outstanding" efficiency report if one was to get ahead.

There were many more competent officers available for command positions in Vietnam than there were commands. Since no dependents were allowed in Vietnam, the tour length was set at one year for morale and other reasons. However, to allow officers to spend their entire tour in command would have restricted the number of command opportunities. Also it was alleged that a one-year tour of command in combat would make too great physical and perhaps emotional demands on an officer. (I doubt it.) Therefore, the command tour was set at six months, with commanders constantly rotating. Those of us who had our own command positions in Vietnam were required to attend changes of command ceremonies for others almost weekly. In time, this became about as interesting as attending the baptism of an infant of distant friends.

Once in command, the aspirant had to look good in a very short period of time, and this is where the problems of careerism were most evident. What happened was that, as one general put it, "There were too many battalion and brigade commanders getting their tickets punched rather than trying to really lead." The stress was on establishing a performance image rather than on achieving positive results.

A great amount of literature has been written on the problems of the United States Army late in the Vietnam War period. Many of these problems, it has been alleged (and I agree), stemmed from careerism, especially as a side effect of the rapid rotation of commanders. One issue involved the false reporting of body counts and the like, which was so corrosive of professional standards. Another effect of the short tour and the race for short-term demonstrable results was a lack of consideration for and indeed an insensitivity toward subordinates, especially enlisted men. Late in the war, this type of superficial leadership was well covered by the press in the form of stories about desertion rates, drug addiction, minor mutinies, and the assassination (or "fragging," if one prefers) of junior officers and noncommissioned officers. It is easy to blame the quality of the enlisted men or the lack of support on the home front for all this. But let's state it straight—the problem, where it existed, was one of ineffective leadership, in large part because many leaders made a career out of their own careers rather than a career out of leading their own units.[2]

Many of the generals who responded to my questionnaire commented on the problem, and one such comment was especially pointed: "I believe the 'can do' philosophy which was considered such a virtue by some senior leaders was often at the expense of the troops. Senior leaders did not see this; they saw only the great 'enthusiasm' of intermediate commanders, especially ambitious lt. colonels and colonels."

The breakdown in discipline manifested by desertions and other matters was most clear to the junior officer who had the problem on his hands. All too often junior officers would "solve" the problem by becoming one of the boys, as a division commander remarked to me. The situation was worse in the rear areas than in combat units, but it was a problem everywhere for the junior officer, made even worse by the deterioration in quality of the junior officers as the war progressed. That was due in part to the continued large number of junior officers required, and in part to the fact that quality young men were hiding from the draft, usually through some legal evasion, such as advanced education.

This deterioration in junior officer leadership was apparently not evident to a majority of the generals, as indicated by responses to the following question:

Junior officer leadership (Capt., Lt.):	*Percentage*
(1) Improved throughout the war	34
(2) Remained about the same throughout the war	30
(3) Deteriorated as the war went on	32
(4) Other or no answer	4

2. Perhaps it should be emphasized that careerism did not originate in Vietnam, but was exacerbated by the situation there. In my opinion it was a product of World War II and, to a lesser extent, the Korean War. Lieutenant colonels unknown in the prewar period emerged as four- and five-star generals. The ambitious officer in the postwar world, with these examples to look to, thought that to get ahead, one had to do everything—command, serve on high-level staffs, and attend school at every echelon of the schooling system. There was scarcely time to get

If nearly a third of the commanding generals were aware of this deterioration, an interesting point is raised. It was put rather sharply by William R. Corson: "By accepting junior officer leadership it knew to be inferior, and by not changing its strategy and tactics to account for this reality, the military hierarchy insured not only a diminished combat effectiveness, but also the creation of other problems totally beyond the ken of the system's leaders at all ranks."[3]

Before discussing the professionalism of the general officers themselves, I want to consider three background variables, significant to the analysis in the concluding chapter but best discussed in the present context. The first of these is West Point. I have noted that about half of the generals in the survey are West Point graduates. West Point and its products are a favorite subject for writers, scholarly and otherwise. Let us recall some of the frequent statements concerning the effect on an individual graduate of the West Point indoctrination system.

First, from the West Point catalog: "The academic curriculum and military training encourages logical analysis, clear and concise expression of considered views, and independent thought and action along with a readiness, developed within the framework of military discipline, to carry out orders without reservation once a decision has been reached." In other words, West Pointers are trained to carry out orders without questioning them. A military virtue, to some extent. However, when combined with the extreme deference which the military give to rank, it is a virtue which may at times lead to unfortunate consequences.

In a July 1967 article in *Newsweek* entitled "West Point Goes to War" this virtue was discussed in a comparative sense. Quoting a West Point graduate speaking about his fellow graduates, the article stated: There is just something about behavior that is drummed into them. Because of their education, they don't ask questions when there is a job to be done. They do it. ROTC people, on the other hand, are inclined to ask 'why?'"

Ellis and Moore, in their important work on West Point, discuss this aspect of the socialization process at the Academy in somewhat

---

acquainted with one job before one had to be angling for the next. For COMUSMACV's opinion on this problem see Westmoreland, *A Soldier Reports*, p. 296.

3. Corson, *Consequences of Failure* (New York, Norton, 1974), p. 84.

broader terms: "He—the cadet—is trained to perform as a 'public servant' who does not question the wisdom or integrity of those in authority. And like much at West Point, this tradition has the sanction of tradition." Again, "Whether they are called company men or team players, or mission-oriented managers, the result is a loyal subordinate who can usually be counted on to acclimate his personality and talents to the job at hand."[4]

Finally, there is the matter of the influence of West Point concepts not only on its own graduates, but through its graduates on the entire Army. This has been noted many times and is aptly summed up by Maureen Mylander: "The real Academy transcends time and place because no graduate ever leaves West Point. He takes it with him. Thus the school's influence extends not only through the sheer number, rank and power of its graduates, but through the force of their belief."[5]

Another background variable is airborne qualification. The rise of the "airborne club" in the Army, beginning just before World War II, is legendary; Matthew Ridgway, Maxwell Taylor, and James Gavin are just a few of the group whose careers were enhanced by being airborne qualified. They in turn assisted following generations of airborne leadership. William Westmoreland, although he did not become airborne until after World War II, was one of these. Although parachute use in Vietnam played little part in the war, a large number of the commanders were airborne qualified. Undoubtedly, Westmoreland selected the best commanders he could and gave little thought to their airborne qualifications, but there is small question that he knew and admired the airborne group.

Whether this group viewed the war differently from their non-airborne colleagues we can leave for the moment. There is one further point to be made, however, and that concerns the airborne qualification itself. It would be erroneous to believe that airborne training changed the outlook of its graduates in this senior group. I agree with William Cockerham that action-oriented individuals self-select into the airborne in response to such inducements as self-identification with an elite unit and the reward of higher status

4. Joseph Ellis and Robert Moore, *School for Soldiers* (New York: Oxford University Press, 1974), pp. 194, 197.
5. *The Generals*, p. 32.

within the military.[6] Cockerham believes further that airborne socialization did not bring about a significant change in individual values and attitudes, but rather that individuals brought their basic values with them into the airborne. This also seems reasonable.

One final variable in the generals' background is branch, especially the differences between Infantry and Armor. Before being promoted to general, all officers have served in one of the branches of the Army. The two maneuver branches, in doctrine and outlook, view combat differently. An officer graduate of Fort Benning, with subsequent tours with the Infantry, would have felt at home in the Vietnam War. It was essentially an infantryman's war. An officer product of Fort Knox and subsequent tours in jobs of the Armor type would probably view the war more critically. Professionally, he would have felt more at home with rapidly moving Armor formations. Patton's great race across France in August 1944 was the apogee of this experience.

The generals experienced some of the difficulties that lower-ranking officers did. There was, for example, the rapid turnover in jobs. "In II Field Force, the most prestigious headquarters with over one hundred maneuverable battalions at the peak of the buildup, generals' tenure averaged 7.6 months."[7] Of the 183 generals who commanded in Vietnam, over half served there as generals (frequently in more than one job) for less than a year, and a quarter for less than eight months. In part, this high rate of turnover was probably unavoidable owing to promotions, new job requirements, and, toward the end, a reduced force structure.

Constant change in command was not the only thing that the generals had in common with some of the lower-ranking officers. Although the questionnaire did not raise issues of professionalism or careerism as they pertained to the generals, there were occasional comments added on the subject. One general was singled out by two respondents, one his superior, and one an adjacent commander, as being guilty of inflating his body counts. In another case, a division commander wrote that his corps-level commander

6. William C. Cockerham, "Selective Socialization: Airborne Training as a Status Passage," *Journal of Political and Military Sociology*, 1 (1973), 215–229.

7. *The Generals*, p. 191. Mylander is citing from a Department of Army study (which, however, ends in 1968).

became very unhappy with him for not being able to produce a high body count on a particular occasion. It seems that the Field Force Commander had reported a major battle to COMUSMACV. It was one of those occasions when the VC simply slipped away, and there *was* no significant body count. All the Force Commander wanted, the division commander said, was to look good for six months "and get out with a clean slate"—a not uncommon desire. Allegations along these lines were not, however, extensive.

A more serious charge concerns the failure of the higher leadership to speak out. Writing in 1973, two young officers stated: "Very few in the officers corps 'stood up to be counted'—on the body count, base camp luxuries, or other legacies of peacetime which followed to Vietnam—legacies of the hypocrisy of 'looking good.' Even more so, many tolerated the quibbling of a reporting system conditioned to tell the commander what he wanted to hear."[8] A lieutenant general wrote on his questionnaire: "I don't think military did itself proud in Vietnam—why didn't the military leaders at the top speak out?"

Observers like Maureen Mylander think that the problem was systemic. "Most generals keep their dissent private," she wrote, "and take what the Army offers for as long as possible. To become a general, and particularly to become a high-ranking one, an officer must conform, avoid error, shun controversy, and forego dissent."[9]

Others feel that the system can and should be changed. I agree. A good example of this group is retired Navy Vice Admiral William P. Mack, former Superintendent of the United States Naval Academy. In his farewell address on August 1, 1975, he raised the issue of the need for dissent within the military. He blamed the American failure in Vietnam on closed minds and the suppression of dissenting opinion at the nation's highest military and political levels. "I will not give them names, but I knew most of these decision makers—in the Pentagon, the State Department, the White House, and in Vietnam. They may have been the best—whatever that means—they may have been bright, but most of them were wrong."

"I knew many who were right on the issues," Admiral Mack continued, "some, more senior, many more, junior, but few of them survived. In those years dissenters were not popular." He went on

8. Bradford and Brown, *The United States Army in Transition*, p. 177.
9. *The Generals*, p. 211.

to stress "the necessity of listening to and protecting the existence of the dissenter, the person who does not necessarily agree with his commander or with popularly held opinion."[10] Let us hope somebody was listening.

Failure to Mobilize the Reserves

Over 90 percent of the generals responding to the survey felt that the manner in which Reserve Forces were employed in the Vietnam War was an error. In a high percentage of the cases the feeling was that they were called up too late (1968), and that they should have been called up in large numbers rather than in the token numbers eventually mobilized.

Many pointed out that all plans for a contingency the size of the Vietnam conflict were based upon a reserve mobilization. Others spoke of the drastic effects on the active forces, world-wide, brought about by the personnel turbulence caused by eight years of operations in Vietnam. Many also felt that the failure to mobilize was one reason the country never got behind the war. Another frequent comment was that the quality of junior officer leadership which the reserves could provide would have prevented lowering OCS standards to the Calley-Medina level. The question then is why the reserves were not called up.

Prior to 1965 there was every reason to believe that a Reserve Force mobilization would occur in the event of any military action on the scale of Vietnam. There had been mobilizations for World War II, the Korean War, and even for the Berlin crisis of 1961. Before World War II, both the National Guard and Army Reserve provided for a large number of units lightly manned—about 50 percent for the Guard, and almost only paper units for the Army Reserve. By the time of the Korean War, Reserve Force units were still only at about 50 percent strength when mobilized. Between the Korean conflict and the Berlin crisis of 1961, the number of reserve units was modified to bring personnel and force structure into closer balance. As a result, mobilization units were at almost 70 percent of strength, the highest achieved in any

10. Excerpted from the Magazine Supplement to the *Army Times*, January 12, 1976.

mobilization up to then. Following the Berlin call-up, units were further improved, so that when the Vietnam mobilization came, units averaged over 85 percent strength.

The Berlin mobilization, no matter how efficiently conducted, did affect to some degree decisions concerning the part the Reserves were to play in the Vietnam War. During the Berlin crisis, unlike previous mobilizations, Reservists were unable to see any clear and present danger to this country. The result was an enormous outcry at having their careers and families disrupted by being called to active duty. Vietnam was not the same as Berlin in many respects, but it was similar to Berlin in regard to skepticism that there was a danger to the United States. It was difficult even for a defense enthusiast to detect imminent danger. Senior civilians in the Pentagon in 1965 who had been around in 1961, and there were many, remembered the problems of that call-up very well, and they were not sanguine about the possibilities of another one.

Whatever the legacy of Berlin, JCS and Service Southeast Asia contingency plans definitely were based on the call-up of the Reserves. For example, the Army's active force structure was uniquely oriented toward combat units; hence many logistic units existed principally in the Reserves. Again, the plans called for mobilizing Reserve training divisions to train new recruits for the Army, this freeing the Active Army Training Center cadres for reassignment. Many other examples could be cited, but the point is that contingency planning viewed the Army Active and Reserves as one force, and war plans were drawn up accordingly.

The basic decision not to mobilize the Reserves was made by President Johnson in July 1965. The deteriorating situation in South Vietnam caused the then new leadership in Saigon— General Thieu, in effect chief of state, and Marshal Ky, Prime Minister—to request large-scale United States ground forces to supplement those introduced in the spring. To look into the situation, Secretary McNamara made one of his many trips to Saigon. On his return to Washington, July 20, he recommended an increase in American troop strength in Vietnam from 75,000 to around 200,000. To accomplish this, he proposed to the President a total increase in the Armed Forces of 600,000 and suggested that 235,000 be obtained by a call-up of the Reserve Forces.[11]

There were, at that time, two methods available to the President to provide Reserve personnel to the Armed Forces. He could ask

11. Johnson, *The Vantage Point*, p. 146.

Congress for a joint resolution authorizing the call-up, or he could declare a national emergency and call as many as one million Reservists for one year. Since no one expected the war to be over in a year, the latter course did not seem practical. Additionally, in 1965 the President did not want to declare a national emergency in regard to events in Vietnam, which were being played in a relatively low key.

A congressional resolution would also pose problems. Earlier hints of a Reserve mobilization indicated some opposition in Congress and the possibility of a major congressional debate. Despite the fact that all who were present when McNamara briefed the President had supported his recommendation on the Reserves, the prospects of a debate in Congress caused the President to have some second thoughts. In a few days it became clear that the Department of Defense was being asked to find ways of getting manpower other than through using the Reserve Forces.

The decision about increasing the troop strength in Vietnam was announced by LBJ in a speech on July 28. The needed manpower would be obtained by increasing the draft quotas. The decision not to call up the Reserves, as McNamara had recommended, was obviously a political one, but it had its own rationale. The use of increased draft quotas provided flexibility in adjusting United States military strength to the level required for a war whose duration and level were not yet known. On the other hand, bringing in the Reserves would tend to be construed as a mobilization. This could be viewed as a significant acceleration of the war not in keeping, perhaps, with the limited aims in Vietnam—at least, not as the United States Government then defined them publicly.[12] In any case, the announcement caught much of the Armed Services leadership by surprise. In Fort Lewis, Washington, for example, the post was already readying barracks for the arrival of the Reserves.

There is another major factor—President Johnson's desire to protect his domestic programs, the "Great Society." This was, as Doris Kearns has pointed out, "to be his monument, his passport to historical immortality." The debate attendant on a full scale Reserve Force call-up, Johnson felt, would have jeopardized his domestic programs, ending his attempt to have both guns and butter. Priorities would have to be defined; and those in Congress

12. William F. Levantrosser, *Congress and the Citizen-Soldier* (Columbus, Ohio State University Press, 1967), p. 226.

opposed to Johnson's programs would have had their opportunity to blunt them.[13]

Military pressure for a call-up of the Reserves did not end with the President's decision of July 1965, however. Late that year and early in the next, General Westmoreland's troop requirements began to exceed the capabilities of the services to provide them without a Reserve call-up. Aside from the manpower needs, General Johnson, the Army Chief of Staff, saw other reasons to employ the Reserves. He felt it might be "an important factor in the reading of the North Vietnamese and the Chinese with respect to our determination to see the war through."[14] He also felt that it might help to unify the country in support of the war effort.

Secretary McNamara perceived that there were many conflicting forces in the country which would work against making a decision at that time for a call-up. There were, first of all, problems with the Fulbright Committee and its hearings, which were nonsupportive of the war. Others felt the country was overextended economically and could not even afford what was already being done. Still others felt that we should not be in Vietnam at all. With all these pressures, McNamara believed that the Administration would have a difficult task to mobilize public opinion sufficiently to support a call-up.

Writing in the spring of 1966, Hanson Baldwin made the case for mobilization.[15] In his critique of the state of the war, Baldwin noted that the decision not to mobilize was a calculated risk on the part of the President. The risk had led to withdrawals of trained troops from Europe and the strategic Reserve in the United States, with the result that no real forces were available for any emergency which might develop outside of Vietnam. He went on to point out great deficiencies in engineering and construction units that could easily be supplied by Reserve units of the exact type needed.

Although Baldwin agreed that regular forces must be mobile and able to handle small contingencies, he felt that by the spring of 1966 expectations of what active forces could accomplish alone were excessive. "The military leaders feel that under McNamara the shift to regular forces has gone too far," he wrote, "and the

13. For a perceptive treatment of this aspect of the problem see Doris Kearns, *Lyndon Johnson and the American Dream* (New York, Harper and Row, 1976), pp. 260–285.

14. *PP*, Vol. 4, p. 314.

15. *The Reporter* (May 19, 1966), pp. 20–23.

potential of mobilization has been downgraded to an extreme." He also believed that mobilizing the Reserves would help to reverse the tide of opposition to the war in Congress and promote national unity. In his view, our failure to mobilize lessened the credibility of our Vietnam policy in the eyes of the Hanoi leadership. Mobilization would clearly signal that we were prepared to stay the course.

By late 1966, withdrawals of equipment from Reserve units to support new activations in the regular forces had degraded the mobilization potential of the Reserve components, but the JCS were still talking in terms of a full mobilization, which would involve almost 700,000 reservists. At this point they were making a two-pronged case for mobilization. First, without mobilizing, they could not both meet Westmoreland's requirements for 1967 and fulfill their commitments to NATO and other areas. Second, only a massive infusion of firepower and manpower into Vietnam would permit termination of the war "in the shortest time with the least cost."[16]

Arguing against the JCS position the following spring, William Bundy, Assistant Secretary of State, felt that an attempt at a mobilization would involve a major debate in Congress. He believed that such a debate would only encourage Hanoi, and that it would be unwise to bring Congress into the matter. And so it went, the JCS holding its position throughout the remainder of 1967 but getting nowhere with the White House or other areas of government. For better or worse, the President and, by now, the Secretary of Defense and congressional leaders had decided that if the war had reached the point of requiring a mobilization, its political costs were inordinate. Domestic constraints, not strategic or tactical military considerations, were dictating American war policy. What finally got the Joint Chiefs their mobilization, small as it was, were two external events that had not been anticipated.

Long-existing tensions between North and South Korea flared up in January 1968. On the 18th of the month some North Korean agents attempted to assassinate the President of South Korea. Five days later, on the 23rd of January, North Korean gunboats seized the United States intelligence ship *Pueblo* off the coast of North Korea. The JCS, previously unsuccessful in persuading the Administration to mobilize the Reserves, now had a new rationale. On

16. *PP*, Vol. 4, p. 395.

January 25 the President directed the Secretary of Defense to call to active duty almost 15,000 Air Force and Navy reservists.[17]

Just six days later, in the early morning hours of January 31, 1968, the Tet Offensive began. The debate within the Administration on a Reserve call-up merged with the debate on how many reinforcements Westmoreland was to receive. The JCS considered three plans to meet the situation; one called for a call-up, the other two did not. The call-up plan was recommended. By this time, Clark Clifford was in charge of making the famous "A to Z reassessment," and the decision on the call-up was deferred until an overall decision on the war was made by the President. In the end, Westmoreland received a small increase (the last) of troop strength, and there was a token call-up of Reserves.

On April 11 the Secretary of Defense announced the order to active duty in May of 24,500 personnel, the bulk of whom were Army personnel. Of these, about 9,000 were earmarked for eventual deployment to Vietnam. There were, however, serious problems with many of these reserve units, as to both their readiness and, in certain instances, their attitude about active service in what was now an unpopular war.

Despite optimistic premobilization estimates of these units, those mobilized had to undergo a full unit training program, once on active duty. In part, this was due to personnel problems, and in part to equipment shortages. Short suspense dates and security had prevented adequate planning for those called up, and this further exacerbated the situation.

Moreover, it was difficult to explain to many reservists the reasons for mobilization, or why particular units were called to active duty and not others. Shortly after the units arrived at their mobilization stations, the Department of the Army received numerous congressional inquiries on behalf of the reservists or their relatives. In part these reflected low readiness to serve, and in part displeasure at their sudden transformation from civilian to military life.

Some units challenged the legality of the call-up. One such was the 1002nd Supply and Service Company, which had its movement

17. In October 1966 the Defense Appropriations Act for Fiscal Year 1967 gave the President an additional option for calling up Reserves, authorizing him to call any Reserve unit to active duty for up to twenty-four months. This authority was effective until June 30, 1968.

to Vietnam held up by Justice William O. Douglas in September 1968. In the end, the Supreme Court denied the plea and declared the mobilization legal, and units earmarked for Vietnam were sent there as rapidly as possible. Most Reserve units that served in Vietnam did well. A few were excellent.

The two Army generals most concerned with the call-up, though in different ways, were General Harold K. Johnson, Army Chief of Staff, and General Westmoreland. In retrospective comments on the war, General Westmoreland expressed his feeling that there never was a point when the President could have called up the Reserves before the Tet Offensive. Prior to that, Westmoreland himself had been ambivalent about a call-up. His thought was that such an action might set loose pressures to disengage prematurely, in order to get the reservists home. Also, after their one-year tours in Vietnam, there would be pressure to release them from active duty, which would be disruptive Army-wide. Viewing the war from Saigon, Westmoreland felt that Tet was dramatic enough to bring the country behind the war effort, as had the Battle of the Bulge in World War II. This, he thought, was the strategic time for the call-up. As we know now, it was already too late, for the will of the country to wage the war had eroded badly. Tet, rather than serving as a rallying point made the nation more determined to get out of Vietnam.

General Johnson's view from Washington was one of concern for the Army world-wide. Its deterioration, brought about by the size of the commitment in Vietnam and the one year tour there, was of serious concern to him. Of all the chiefs, he was probably the most insistent on the need for the Reserves. He felt that the main problem preventing a call-up was the legacy of the 1961 Berlin call-up and the ensuing outcry. Another argument frequently made in response to his requests for the Reserves was that they were a "wasting asset"—they were only good when not called up, primarily for their deterrent value. That kind of reasoning prompts a question. If the Reserves cannot be used when needed, why base all plans on their use? Furthermore, if they cannot be used except in all-out war, are they really worth the effort and cost at the scale on which they are maintained? As General Johnson once remarked, we are "feeding the horse but never taking him out of the barn."

The foregoing considerations were not lost on the professional reservists. In August 1970 Secretary of Defense Melvin Laird was induced to sign a memorandum to all of the military departments on "Support for Guard and Reserve Forces." In effect, the memorandum said that in the future the Reserves could expect to be mobilized from the first in any national emergency.

Although the purpose of the memorandum was to provide a basis for an effective Reserve force, there is question whether it was purely rhetorical, designed to keep critics from questioning the need for a large-scale Reserve. When, for example, would a national emergency be declared? Would such an emergency be credible in a situation like Vietnam, which was not central to United States security? If not, would the Reserves be available? In view of the Vietnamese experience, some healthy skepticism seems in order.

Adversary Relations with the Media

The worst feature of the war was the fracturing of our society. This took the form we all know so well; heavily slanted, anti-administration and anti-military reporting in the news media. . . . Hanoi was able, through our press, to monitor closely . . . the situation respecting U.S. morale and willingness to continue the fight. The record was good until America itself lost much of its will to fight and the politicians and press began their program of villification.—General Hamilton H. Howze, U.S. Army, Retired.[18]

The camera, the typewriter, the tape recorder are very effective weapons in this war—weapons too often directed not against the enemy, but against the American people. These weapons have a far greater potential for defeating us than the rockets or artillery used against our men in Vietnam. In a free society, in which the right of dissent is a sacred principle, an enemy has boundless opportunity to manipulate our emotions.—Lt. General Lewis W. Walt, U.S. Marine Corps, Retired.[19]

18. Howze, "Vietnam . . . an Epilogue," *Army*, 25 (1975), 15.
19. Walt, *Strange War—Strange Strategy* (New York, Funk and Wagnalls, 1970), p. 200.

Generals Howze and Walt are not the only high-level officials, military and civilian, who have taken the media to task for their handling of the Second Indochinese War. In examining the role of the media in the war, it is well to keep in mind that the American home front has seldom been highly enthusiastic about wars, except at the very beginning. Thereafter—and this is true of all American wars except World Wars I and II—opposition has developed in Congress, the press, and the pulpit. In part, this can be attributed to the media of the day, in part to economic problems, and in part to a perceived lack of progress over time, along with continuing draft calls and mounting casualties.

In an interesting study of the polls, Louis Harris has outlined the changing mood of the public toward the Vietnam war.[20] There was early public support, followed by a serious drop during the episodes, including the Buddhist self-immolations, which led to the assassination of President Diem. Johnson had slightly more support after Diem, and it swung to 85 percent following the Gulf of Tonkin affair in August 1964. Although large numbers of Americans wanted some kind of negotiated settlement, LBJ had good public support in 1965 through the initiation of the bombing and the initial American troop commitments. By December 1965 he had 65 percent support for his handling of the war—a point he never reached again. From July 1966 until the end of his term of office, support went downhill. Subsequently, public reaction to the Tet Offensive sealed the domestic verdict on the war. The next month President Johnson announced his decision not to run again for President. What was the role of the media?

In the early 1960's how to handle the media, at least in the field, was primarily a problem for the government of Vietnam, but since the Vietnamese controlled ARVN actions, United States military advisers were occasionally involved in cooperating with GVN attempts to stifle news. President Diem's view of the role of the press was not that of the United States. In any case, United States advisers were involved enough to become identified with the South Vietnamese in repression of bad news.

Not only was Diem taking action against certain elements of the press from Saigon, but the United States Military Assistance Group, then headed by General Harkins, was also involved. Har-

20. Harris, *The Anguish of Change* (New York, Norton, 1973), chapters 5, 6.

kins' optimism about the progress of the ARVN and of the war in general was a major issue. Certain reporters, at least in the areas with which they were familiar, knew better on both counts. Another issue in the advisory days of 1962 were the attempts on the part of United States officials to conceal the extent to which "advisers" were performing combat duties.

The matter was not confined to Saigon, but the issue in Washington in the advisory days was not so much between the government and the American editors, who generally sided with the officials, as between government officials and the correspondents in Vietnam. A cable from the State Department to Saigon warned against providing transportation for correspondents who might produce undesirable stories. Furthermore, warnings were to be given the press that continued criticism of the Diem regime would have an adverse effect on United States relations with that government.[21]

In January 1963 there occurred an action the aftermath of which destroyed good relations between the press and the military in South Vietnam—the battle at Ap Bac in the northern Delta between an armored element of the ARVN Seventh Division and a Vietcong unit. It was a disaster for the ARVN; yet American headquarters in Saigon referred to it as a victory. The American and British correspondents who were there knew otherwise, and reported what they knew. Some stories quoted John Paul Vann, then a lieutenant colonel, on the high quality of the VC and the cowardly actions of the ARVN.[22]

The reaction of the American Mission was violent—the correspondents were "inexperienced," "unsophisticated," "irresponsible," and their reports "sensationalized." In Washington, reports coming from field correspondents were characterized as "emotional" and "inaccurate." Halberstam, in particular, was singled out to the point where President Kennedy tried unsuccessfully to have him reassigned.[23]

21. Philip Knightley, *The First Casualty* (New York, Harcourt, Brace, Jovanovich, 1975), p. 376.

22. Stories were filed by Halberstam of the *New York Times*, Browne of the Associated Press, Sheehan of United Press International, and Turner of Reuters. A good account of the Ap Bac incident is in Halberstam, *The Making of a Quagmire* (New York, Random House, 1964), pp. 145–162.

23. Knightley, pp. 378–380.

After Ap Bac, correspondents, convinced that the Mission was lying to them, relied on their own sources—in fact, withdrew into their own community.[24] It should be noted that they were not questioning the propriety of the American presence; that was to come later. No doubt existed at this point regarding the premises of United States involvement or of its ability to prevail. There were questions about the South Vietnamese ability to fight and about the tactics being employed, but as yet the correspondents were not raising the big question of whether we should be there at all.

One legacy of this early period was that any form of strong press control became impossible. The press formulated its own guidelines, such as not publishing details of military operations until the Military Assistance Command had released them. Subsequently, attempts were made to rebuild the credibility of the United States Information Offices, but without any notable success so far as projecting a favorable image of United States efforts is concerned.

The Pentagon Papers are replete with references to the press and the reporting on the war. In August 1963 a report from Halberstam in the *New York Times* indicated that the situation in the Delta had deteriorated seriously for government forces. That fall when McNamara and Taylor went to Saigon, one quarter of their 135-page fact book was devoted to refuting the allegations of field correspondents. There were 24 pages on Halberstam's Delta report alone.[25]

In early February 1965, just before the United States ground force commitment, McGeorge Bundy in a report to the President on a trip to Vietnam touched on the subject. "U.S. policy within Vietnam is mainly right and well-directed," he wrote. "None of the special solutions or criticisms put forward with zeal by individual reformers in government or in the press is of major importance, and many of them are flatly wrong."[26]

Probably the best example of high-level misleading of the press and public occurred in connection with the build-up of American

24. There were other reporters who thought the war was going well. They were not regularly based in Vietnam but made periodic visits and could usually be counted on to be supportive of United States efforts and results. Examples: Marguerite Higgins, Joseph Alsop, and Frank Conniff.
25. *PP*, Vol. 3, pp. 23 ff.
26. Ibid., p. 309.

forces in the spring of 1965. The idea was to give the appearance that there had been no change in policy. The Administration would let things happen—in other words, from a public point of view, back into the war. Such were the contents of National Security Action Memorandum of April 6, 1965.[27] This approach first eroded and then destroyed President Johnson's credibility with the public far more than any action of the media.

Press relations under Westmoreland were a great deal better than under Harkins, but eventually Tet 68 destroyed his credibility too. Speaking on the eve of Tet in November 1967, before the National Press Club, Westmoreland painted a rosy picture. Conjuring up the statistics of the Measurement of Progress system, he indicated steady progress. He stated, in fact, that withdrawal of American troops could begin in 1969 (which they did, but under different conditions). No doubt, when he made his prediction, the election of 1968 was in his mind, and he straddled the issue rather than get involved by predicting during an election year the beginning of a withdrawal that might or might not occur.

It was in this rosy atmosphere that the American people turned on their television sets at the end of January and early February 1968, to view the Tet Offensive. What they saw was shocking beyond belief. Instead of victory, there seemed to be a new war going on. A group of VC commandos was briefly ensconced on the ground of the United States Embassy in the heart of Saigon. How, they wondered, was this possible? What in the world was happening?

A shocker of a different sort occurred a few days later in the streets of Saigon. In the course of the fighting, the Chief of the National Police, Nguyen Ngoc Loan, executed a captured VC officer with a revolver pointed at the man's head. As it turned out, the event was recorded by both a still camera and a TV camera. Whatever the justification for the execution, it was an act of cruelty which did not help the world image of the South Vietnamese at a critically important time for them.

Later, General Westmoreland was to make some complaints about the media coverage of the Tet Offensive, including the related action taking place simultaneously at Khe Sanh in the northern Corps area. Westmoreland felt that the manner in which the press handled the story gave the impression of a defeat for the

27. Ibid., p. 703.

United States, whereas in reality it was a military victory. In his words, "The attitude on the part of the American reporters undoubtedly contributed to the psychological victory the enemy achieved in the United States. . . . In the race to drain every possible sensation . . . reporters made little apparent effort to check facts, while basking in the praise of their home offices for their speed in beating the opposition."[28]

At the time, the General was concerned about how to control what was being reported. In a message to the Commander in Chief of the Pacific, he shared that officer's worry about "the amount of information in the press of aid to the enemy," and was considering "withdrawing one correspondent's accreditation" for a violation of ground rules regarding national security matters. Furthermore, he was planning to limit the access of reporters to certain key spots in the northern part of the country. By return message, the Pacific Commander applauded his actions, which had closed the flow of intelligence information that was of value to the enemy.

Although there had been television crews in Korea, Vietnam was the first televised war in the sense that there was daily, systematic coverage, by means of satellite transmission, by all major networks to over 800 television stations throughout the United States. Because of the importance of this medium in portraying the war, some commentary on it is in order.

As the war dragged on, Americans formed an opinion of the war derived in good part from daily television scenes of Army or Marine forces constantly in action, with helicopters landing in jungle clearings, troops rushing into the jungle, bodies or wounded being loaded on helicopters for evacuation. In between, there were exhibitions of American firepower by artillery and air, including napalm.

Not all broadcasts fitted this pattern, of course. There were dramatic moments which had a striking effect on the public. One of the most famous was Morley Safer's CBS broadcast from the village of Cam Ne in August 1965. Cam Ne was a village from which the Marines had allegedly been receiving fire from the VC. By chance, Safer went along on an operation, which he soon discovered was going to level the village. There was in reality no combat to film since there was no return fire from the village. What Safer did film

28. Westmoreland, *A Soldier Reports*, p. 325. He is highly critical of the media handling of the war; see pp. 66, 163, 419, and 422.

was a Marine lighting a straw hut with a cigarette lighter, and the general burning of the village.

The impact of this event, coming early in the period of American ground commitment, was dramatic. Much of the reaction was directed against CBS for showing the film, including a call from LBJ to the president of the network, but the incident had made its mark. War was no longer a glorious distant thing; it was American boys burning down villages while you watched in your own living room.

There was an impact also from the collective reporting over time by well-known TV news personalities like Walter Cronkite. Cronkite went to Vietnam during the Tet Offensive in 1968 to form his own opinion of the situation. Because he was so well known and the image he had built up was supportive of the war to that point, what he had to say would be important. After his trip, Cronkite did a news special on the war. In a quiet way, it, too, was a shocker. Here was one of America's most respected newscasters, not some young war critic like Halberstam, saying that it was time to think of getting out—our approach in Vietnam was not going to work. It had its effect on the public and perhaps on the bureaucracy, too.

From among the many stories competing for prime time on television news, choices had to be made. Because only a limited time could be allowed for coverage of the war, emphasis was on action to catch the viewers' attention. Therefore, if the choice lay between a combat scene and pacification progress on a pig farm in Hau Nghia Province, the combat scene won. It proved, in fact, impossible to replicate the war on television, especially one as complex as this one, and what came out were bits and pieces selected for their appeal to primetime viewers.

This was not necessarily the fault of the reporter in Vietnam, who might film and write a thirty-minute script on some action and advise on how it should be used, only to have it cut in New York to ninety seconds. Newspapers and magazines have similar problems, but not to the acute degree of television.

The producer, too, had constraints. Jay Epstein, in a provocative and interesting book, points out that news programs must maintain their audience.[29] The news must be so constituted as to prevent channel switching. To maintain that audience, news executives op-

29. Edward Jay Epstein, *News from Nowhere* (New York, Random House, 1973).

erate with the following assumptions: interest is maintained through easily recognizable images; potential or actual conflict is more interesting than placid scenes; and the viewer's span of attention is so limited that action rather than discussion is required.

Finally, as Epstein indicates, the level of news journalism is fixed by limitations of resources of time, money, and manpower available to the news divisions. The problem then is not one of good or bad personnel, but of the very structure of television broadcasting.

One would expect the military managers of the war to have a negative attitude toward media coverage of events in or concerning that tragedy. Aside from problems of waging the war itself, there are more fundamental reasons. The traditional authoritarian nature of military services requires a tight control of all events, including news distribution. The professional expertise of officers concerning military operations permits them to be more critical of news coverage of such matters than civilians. Also, their deep involvement in military matters causes them to evaluate the treatment by media of matters concerning the military.

Beginning with COMUSMACV, the military had a negative orientation toward media coverage of events during the Second Indochinese War.[30] In general, Westmoreland felt that the media representatives, with a few exceptions, had no appreciation of the fundamentals of military tactics and strategy and were politically oriented, in that they were interested in stories with a political slant.[31] If so, that should not be surprising, for the Vietnamese War, like all wars, was being waged for political purposes.

A case in point is Westmoreland's discussion of Jonathan Schell's coverage in *The New Yorker* of the destruction of the village of Ben Suc in January 1967, in connection with operation Cedar Falls. As Westmoreland points out, the VC were so entwined with certain villages that the only way to control them was "to remove the people and destroy the village."[32] Schell criticized the action, including the shabby treatment of refugees, but his central point

30. As previously mentioned, Westmoreland retained a fair degree of credibility with the press until his April 1967 visit to the United States and his optimistic speech to Congress. Reporters suspected from this point on that he was a tool of LBJ, and many no longer wrote favorable stories about him.

31. *A Soldier Reports*.

32. Ibid., p. 152.

was that destroying villages and creating refugees was no way to win a counterinsurgency war. He proved to be correct.

Westmoreland is especially critical of the manner in which the media created over a period of time an "aura of defeat." This, he says, "coupled with the vocal antiwar elements, profoundly influenced timid officials in Washington."[33] On another level, he deplores the leaks in Washington to the media, which denied the United States the advantages of flexibility, surprise, and strategic deception. President Johnson himself felt he was mistaken not to have imposed some form of censorship on the media early in the war.[34] Westmoreland considered censorship in Vietnam when American ground forces were first committed, but abandoned the idea as impracticable.

Westmoreland's generals shared his negative view of the performance of the news media in Vietnam. That they would have such a view is not surprising, but the intensity of their feelings is: 89 percent negative toward the press, and 91 percent negative toward television. On only one other matter in the survey, the quality of ARVN, was a consensus so nearly approached. It should be noted that the different wording of the two negative questions on each medium indicates a far deeper negative orientation toward television than toward the press:

Newspaper coverage of the war was   *Percentage*
  (1) Generally responsible, and played an important
      role in keeping the United States informed   8
  (2) Uneven. Some good, but many irresponsible   51
  (3) On the whole tended to be irresponsible and
      disruptive of United States efforts in Vietnam   38
  (4) Other or no answer   3

Television coverage of the war was
  (1) Good for American people to see actual scenes
      of fighting about when they occurred   4
  (2) Probably not a good thing in balance because
      such coverage tends to be out of context   39

33. Ibid., p. 410.
34. *Time* (June 28, 1971), p. 15. Secretary McNamara (one of the respondents informs me) in his occasional private anger at press revelations demanded censorship.

(3) Not a good thing, since there was a tendency to go
for the sensational, which was counterproductive
to the war effort   52
(4) Other or no answer   5

There was a great deal of commentary on these questions. It can be grouped into clusters. Several of the respondents felt that the reporters had made up their minds in advance that going into Vietnam was a mistake and were out to prove their point. Many generals attributed a lack of support of the war by the American people to the media. One senior general said that the media conducted "a psychological warfare campaign against the United States policies in Vietnam that could not have been better done by the enemy."

A large number of respondents commented on the media's representation of the war, some saying that the reporters simply did not understand the war, and in other cases that reporting was distorted for effect. In some instances editors at home were blamed for distorting stories or writing misleading headlines. A former Chief of Staff studied combat photography closely and was convinced that much of it was staged. One Division Commander tells of seeing a telegram from one of the major TV networks to a field reporter in his area which read, "Get footage of American soldiers misbehaving."

Not all of the generals were critical of the media. A minority saw shortcomings in the military's handling of reporting the progress in the war. One respondent put it this way: "We placed too much emphasis on the positive, and were over-sensitive to criticism, while engaging in false reporting to cover up setbacks. This, in time, led to our losing credibility."

The media themselves have engaged in a good deal of retrospective assessment of their role in the Vietnam War. One form is the military-media conference held each year at the Naval War College, beginning in 1971. The exchange has been open on both sides. Philip Geyelin, a Pulitzer Prize winner, was especially pointed in his remarks. One of his central points was that the military leadership—and the civilian, for that matter—was less than frank with the public and the press. Comparing Vietnam to Watergate, he described it as a course of action which depended for its success on concealing its true nature from the press and the people.[35] Geyelin went on to state that the military was unrealistic in not expecting the press to inquire deeply into a war that was taking a heavy toll in casualties and resources. In a separate critique Bernard Brodie went one step farther, pointing out that managing information is systemic to the military, and that from 1961 to 1971 the entire Vietnam policy was based upon "doctored" information.[36]

Another type of commentary attempts to define what the role of an American journalist should be during a war. Richard Harwood says: "Even in a war the reporter has an absolute duty to his craft to seek the discipline of detachment and neutrality. If he sees himself as an agent of American government, as a promoter of American policies, he ceases to be a journalist and becomes instead a propagandist."[37]

Neil Sheehan, speaking at the Naval War College in 1970, went even further than Harwood by calling for a protagonist relationship between the news media and the government. S. L. A. Marshall, long-time writer on military affairs, subsequently took him to task for that view, believing it "less a conceit than an illusion."[38]

Another cluster of commentary by journalists is highly critical of media performance in Vietnam for failing to ask the right questions soon enough. In Knightley's words, "Clearly, those charged with the responsibility of informing the United States public about Vietnam had not fulfilled their task. . . . Vietnam created a challenge that few correspondents were able to meet."[39]

In a highly critical article in the *Columbia Journalism Review*, Fred W. Friendly, former president of CBS news, felt that the mistakes made by journalists "almost outran those of the statesmen." The media, he charged, never asked the big questions and never challenged the assumptions on which the war was based,

35. Geyelin's talk at the 1974 conference, "The Role of the Press in an Open Society," is contained in the *Naval War College Review*, 27 (March-April 1975), 3–7.

36. Bernard Brodie, *War and Politics* (New York, Macmillan, 1973), p. 213.

37. Richard Harwood, "Vietnam War. Reporter's Mission," *Washington Post*, March 9, 1971.

38. Sheehan's remarks are in the *Naval War College Review*, 23 (February 1971), and Marshall's are in the April 1971 issue.

39. *The First Casualty*, p. 402.

especially in the early days of United States intervention.[40] Sheehan believes that the media have been given too much credit for influencing events during the Vietnam War. They were, he said, much more "reactive" than "originative"—more reflective of sensed public attitude than responsible for creating new public attitudes toward the war. With Friendly he believes that "we never really did ask any of the basic questions about policy."[41]

I think he is right. Perhaps we should leave it there, with one more comment. A shrewd observer of the press and the war once told me that the importance of the press in swaying public opinion was a myth, fostered by the press to increase its importance. But, he added, it was of importance to the government to perpetuate the myth. In that way, it could be said by government officials that it was not the real situation in Vietnam that the public eventually reacted against, but rather the press portrayal of that situation.

40. Fred W. Friendly, "TV at the Turning Point," *Columbia Journalism Review*, 9 (Winter 1970–71), 13–20.

41. Unpublished manuscript, Military-Media Conference, Naval War College, November 24, 1975.

Terminating the War

Changing Context and Objectives

In the 1968 presidential election campaign, candidate Richard Nixon stated that he had a plan to end the war in Vietnam. As it turned out, the "plan" was embryonic. There had been planning within the bureaucracy on what to do about the war as early as the rump Johnson Administration—after Johnson's March 31st announcement that he would not be a candidate for President.

At that time sections of the Pentagon bureaucracy were no longer talking of winning. Concessions openly discussed within the Office of Secretary of Defense were cession of the two northern provinces of South Vietnam to the North and formation of a coalition government with the Viet Cong in the South. No such views were held by the United States bureaucracy in Saigon, however. Their notions of victory prevailed, although as 1968 wore on, it was increasingly apparent that time was running out fast on the American side.

In the January 1969 issue of *Foreign Affairs* there was an article entitled "The Vietnam Negotiations," written by Henry Kissinger, who was soon to be National Security Adviser to the new president. Kissinger felt that the American objectives should be "1) to bring about a staged withdrawal of external forces, North Vietnamese and American, 2) thereby to create a maximum incentive for the contending forces in South Vietnam to work out a political agreement."[1]

1. The article was written before Kissinger was appointed to his new post, and it was too late to recall it after he was. For a classical critique of it see Bernard Brodie, *War and Politics* (New York, Macmillan, 1973), pp. 197 ff.

It was with such conflicting views in the bureaucracy that the Nixon Administration took office in January 1969. The Administration's only pledge was to end the war and secure United States withdrawal. At this point no one, including Nixon, conceived that it would take four years to accomplish that objective.[2]

On the first day of the new Administration, the first National Security Study Memorandum (NSSM 1), addressed to interested parts of the bureaucracy, posed twenty-eight questions about the situation in Vietnam. They ranged the gamut from purely military matters to political and economic problems.[3] No attempt was made to obtain a consensus among agencies; rather, they were requested to note their differences of opinion, and the reasons therefor.

Within the Defense Department four officials, three of whom were military, set about the task of answering the questions by means of input from various parts of the Defense bureaucracy. Other departments used their own techniques for preparing responses. Apparently the most difficult point to make was that the agencies were not required to produce a consensus response.

The responses showed agreement on some matters and substantial differences on others. General agreement was obtained, however, on the following matters: The Republic of Vietnam could not in the foreseeable future stand up to both the Viet Cong and the North Vietnamese forces. It was also not clear that the government could stand up to peaceful competition from the National Liberation Front alone. Enemy forces were intact or capable of being refurbished, although the VC was not up to the level of their pre-Tet 1968 capability.

There were disagreements among the agencies which constituted roughly two schools of thought. On one side was the military's, from Washington to Saigon and the American Embassy there. This was the optimistic school. The other group, consisting of the Office of the Secretary of Defense, the CIA, and the State Department, was much more pessimistic about the future. The optimists held to the beliefs that had governed them all along. Friendly military operations were, they felt, gaining momentum.

2. General Westmoreland points out that from this point on, "No longer did initiative come from the American command in Saigon; it came from the White House and Dr. Kissinger." A *Soldier Reports* (New York, Doubleday, 1976), p. 386.

3. Excerpts from NSSM I were contained in the *New York Times* (April 26, 1972), p. 16.

The South Vietnamese forces were increasingly effective. Gains in pacification were real and would hold up. Victory, however, was not yet in sight. The pessimists felt that there was essentially a stalemate. Furthermore, no amount of friendly effort within the constraints of this war could bring victory over the other side. A gloomy view prevailed within this group as to the future of ARVN, and apparent gains in pacification were considered fragile indeed. In effect, not only was victory not in sight, but it never would be. The only feasible solution was compromise.

By early April the initial decisions had been made by the President, and he set forth his guidelines for "Vietnamizing" the war. The Secretary of Defense was placed in overall charge of the program, which was to begin on the first of July 1969. A massive effort to upgrade South Vietnamese forces, accompanied by phased withdrawals of United States forces, would be instituted. Completion would depend on how things went in Vietnam. The earliest that United States combat efforts could be terminated was the end of 1970, and the latest, the end of 1972.

Three themes seemed to dominate Nixon's strategy on Vietnam during this protracted withdrawal of almost four years: (1) keep accelerating the United States withdrawal under the rationale that Vietnamizing the war was working; (2) continue to negotiate; and (3) take no action that would seem to violate American "honor."[4]

Regardless of the domestic and political pressures to end the war, Nixon apparently felt strongly that the way the war finally ended would have an enduring impact on American foreign-policy initiatives in the future. If things went wrong, he told a gathering of United States officials in Bangkok in July 1969, a strong isolationist sentiment would be engendered among the American public. He may have been right. Officials in Washington, however, judged that the President was lacking in firmness, and at times different principals had different views as to just what his major policies were. Henry Kissinger became the key adviser on Vietnamization. The Secretary of State, William Rogers, did not work directly with the President on this issue and seemed to have little interest in what was actually happening in Vietnam.

Secretary of Defense Laird wanted the United States out of Vietnam as rapidly as possible for domestic political reasons. In the

4. Louis Harris, *The Anguish of Change* (New York, W. W. Norton, 1973), p. 71.

early stages of his administration of the Pentagon, however, he was reluctant to confront the military directly. Westmoreland, then a member of the Joint Chiefs, felt that Laird appeared to distrust the Chiefs.[5] In any case, by the time Vietnamization was under way, the Chiefs had lost some of their credibility with civilian defense officials because of their previous positions and their understandable reluctance to proceed rapidly with the withdrawal.

By the time the Vietnamization plan was announced in 1969, the attitude of the South Vietnamese people can best be described as war weariness. They had reached a state where the desire to be rid of the war was more important than any desire to defeat the Viet Cong or the North Vietnamese. Even among the South Vietnamese establishment there was an apathy that frequently manifested itself in an acknowledgment that the military solution was probably not going to work. This was not true at the highest levels, where by 1969 President Thieu was, or at least appeared to be, firmly in control. In fact, by this time Thieu was exhibiting certain Diemist tendencies. No thought of accommodation with the NLF was seriously considered, and the military and rightist factions were closely allied to hold together the fragile governmental structure. In official utterances Thieu seemed to display ambivalence. Generally he was strongly anti-Communist: "No coalition government; no neutrality; no participation of Communists in politics; no territory conceded to the Communists." On other occasions, as time went on, he admitted to a willingness to allow some Communist participation—say, in elections.

With this conflict of aims—between a Washington bent on extracting itself from the war as soon as possible and an ambivalent Vietnamese government—the Military Assistance Command increasingly found itself involved from 1969 onward. The key man was General Creighton W. Abrams, Westmoreland's Deputy from the spring of 1967, who had succeeded him in the summer of 1968. It was almost as though another U. S. Grant had shuffled into the major United States military position of the day—so different were his external characteristics from the spit and polish air exuded by his predecessor.

Abrams had been a household word in the American Army since World War II. He had achieved his fame in Europe with the 4th Armored Division and especially as a tank battalion commander.

5. Westmoreland, *A Soldier Reports*, p. 387.

Personally commended by George Patton, Abe was widely considered a comer, although he seemed always a step behind his classmate Westmoreland on the star ladder.

An officer who kept his own counsel, Abrams was admired by his many acquaintances for his soundness of judgment. As a staff officer and commander he stuck to essentials, and within the military framework he arrived at logical and pragmatic solutions to problems. If anyone could have made Vietnamization work (no one could, of course), it would have been Abe.[6] On one matter he was extremely cautious, and that was in dealing with the press. He recognized Westmoreland's mistakes in making or implying predictions about the war. His own policy was to let the facts speak for themselves. In all probability he undermanaged the news; some felt he went to an extreme from Westmoreland.

Abrams' main task was to extricate the American expeditionary force at the same time that the burden of the war was being shifted to the South Vietnamese forces. In his first year or so he moved his forces away from an enemy-oriented strategy toward one focused on the security of the friendly population and the neutralization of the Viet Cong infrastructure. In this he was partly successful. Organizational inertia and perceptions that success was just around the corner made it difficult at first to bring about changes. In time, as the American presence declined, it became easier.

Vietnamization

In early April 1969, Presidential planning guidance on Vietnamization was set forth in National Security Study Memorandum Number 36, which directed "the preparation of a specific timetable for Vietnamizing the war," covering "all aspects of U.S. military, para-military, and civilian involvement in Vietnam, including combat and combat support forces, advisory personnel, and all forms of equipment." One assumption was that United States

6. Westmoreland tells of Abrams' tendency to lose his temper at conferences—shouting and pounding on the table, his face flushed with anger. I never saw this characteristic, but I tend to agree with Westmoreland that it was probably a dialectical stratagem. See A Soldier Reports, p. 222.

withdrawals would be unilateral—that is, there would be no comparable North Vietnamese reduction, which meant that, if this proved to be true, in the end the South Vietnamese would have to take on both the Viet Cong and North Vietnamese.

Withdrawals were to be made on a "cut and try" basis. Periodically General Abrams was to make assessments of the enemy and friendly situations. These assessments were to be the basis for the next phase of redeployment of United States units. In time, however, these assessments—or at least their outcome in terms of announced redeployments—were influenced more by American domestic considerations than by the actual situation in South Vietnam.

Although the continuing assumption by South Vietnamese forces of more military responsibility was clearly central, there was a lot more involved in Vietnamization. What was also needed was a stronger and more viable political and economic apparatus throughout the country. How one puts that kind of improvement on a timetable is hard to say, but that was the objective.

The program officially began on July 1, 1969. It was evident from the outset that two critical problem areas would determine the eventual outcome: the political leadership and the military leadership. Although most Vietnamese had little confidence that either Thieu or Ky could develop a wide political base, they felt that there was no choice but to retain them. Eventually the Thieu-Ky government became the Thieu government, but the problem remained the same to the end—no broad base of political support.

As for the problem of military leadership, most Vietnamese despaired that anything could be done to get rid of the incompetent, inefficient, and corrupt among ARVN general officers. Only a handful of the generals had the confidence of lower-ranking officers, who in turn felt that the generals were more concerned about their own welfare than that of the country.

By the spring of 1970 most observers felt that a point of diminishing returns had been reached in regard to the improvement of the ARVN, except perhaps in the field of logistics. Defensively the ARVN was performing well, but with enormous American fire support. The rampant corruption made any chance of leadership improvement slight; and for the same reason, the possibility of ARVN becoming an instrument of social progress was almost nonexistent—a distressing fact in a revolutionary war.

In 1970 a high percentage of senior ARVN officers felt that they could hold their own against enemy forces only if significant United States air, artillery, helicopter, and medical support continued. A common concern was that United States withdrawals would be too rapid. On my next to last day in Vietnam in May 1970, I had luncheon with an ARVN general who spoke fluent English. His theme was that the United States was leaving too hastily and the chances of ARVN making it were slight. At that time he was considered unduly pessimistic. Now we know better.

The events of May 1970 involving the Cambodian incursion increased the optimism of both American and South Vietnamese officials. In March 1970 Prince Sihanouk was overthrown and the Lon Nol government came to power in Cambodia. For years the enemy sanctuaries and supply caches in the border areas of that country had been a problem for the Americans and South Vietnamese. Now there was a government in Phnom Penh that would permit something to be done about it. By April, ARVN forces in the III and IV Corps tactical zones were mounting operations into the former Cambodian sanctuaries. With American support, at least up to the border's edge, these were fairly successful operations, especially in terms of destroying enemy supplies of various kinds, and soon the notion of American forces participating in cross-border operations began to be considered. The military advantages of such operations would be impressive. North Vietnamese stocks brought close to the border, previously an immune area, were vulnerable to such operations. Most important, once they were captured or destroyed, the enemy effort would be set back perhaps a year, since their resupply down the Ho Chi Minh trail would be long and tedious. Vietnamization would have gained time. In the areas in which the Americans would participate, the operations would be difficult and considered beyond ARVN capability.

The decision was made by President Nixon to conduct the operations, commencing April 30, 1970, Vietnam time, in III Corps and later in II Corps to the north. Militarily successful—at least in III Corps—they were regarded as a disaster on the home front. This was partly because of an inadequate television presentation by the President, explaining the rationale for the operations. More important, however, was the fact that there was no domestic support for any expansion of the war, however temporary and however compelling for military reasons. That spring will always be remembered as the time of the Kent State shootings, the closing down of the nation's campuses, and the final public ultimatum to the President to get out of the war.

Secretary Laird, the President's manager of Vietnamization, had meanwhile established a Vietnamese Task Force in International Security Affairs, the Pentagon's "State Department." Its purpose was to keep the Secretary informed and to serve as a prod to the defense bureaucracy to expedite the United States withdrawal. Before long the Task Force was living in its own statistical world. Success in Vietnamization was measured not by the body count but by its own litany, which was the reverse of the build-up period: troop-strength reduction ahead (but not too far ahead) of Presidential goals, percentage reduction of United States maneuver battalions, percentage decrease in Americans killed, increased percentage of Vietnamese Air Force sorties flown, etc. What did it all mean? Who knew? Who knows now? At least it sounded as though the Vietnamese were taking over the war, and it provided an apparently professional military basis for a political withdrawal.

To be sure, there were misgivings on the part of many officials, especially over the durability of ARVN improvements. Some doubted whether their increased capability could be maintained as the United States withdrawal schedule continued and increasing burdens were transferred to the Vietnamese. The Communist forces, for their part, seemed convinced that the gains of the other side were transient and the proper approach was to keep a fairly low profile, outlast the United States, and then contend with the South Vietnamese government.

During ARVN operations into Cambodia in the spring of 1970, American strength was about 430,000. By the following February, when ARVN was gearing up for cross-border operations into Laos against the Ho Chi Minh Trail, the figure was about 300,000. There were, however, other more important problems than military strength. The Senate in December 1970 had through the appropriations process prohibited American ground troops from operating outside of Vietnam. Although the American forces provided logistical, air, and firepower support from within Vietnam, advisers were not able to accompany the South Vietnamese forces.

At first things went well for ARVN on Operation Lam Son 719, as it was known. They did reach and interdict the North Vietnamese supply trails. At this point Thieu issued an impetuous "on to Tchepone" order. It proved to be rhetoric, and poor rhetoric at that, because the North Vietnamese counterattacked and dev-astated the ARVN. Cut off from their "advisers," the South Viet-namese were unable to arrange adequate fire support (a problem they never solved) or resupply. They were able to withdraw but looked bad, even though they had severely damaged enemy logis-tic facilities in the operation. That ended any grand notions of major ARVN offensives. Henceforth they would function solely as a defensive force.

Actually, at this point many in Washington and Saigon were wondering if we had created the proper kind of ARVN. Many doubted whether the force was supportable over a long period of time. There was first the manpower drain of the entire armed forces on Vietnam's very small, skilled manpower base. About half the country's able-bodied men were in the military. Then there was the sheer cost and the logistic problems. Would the United States Congress continue indefinitely to support this large and ex-pensive force? Some began to have doubts by 1971, but they were not powerful enough to move the American or Vietnamese bu-reaucracy.

Thoughout 1972, as the Vietnamese forces "improved," United States strength dropped. Beginning at somewhat under 200,000, by year's end it was under 30,000. Two events dominated the scene: the Communist Easter offensive in the spring, and the negotiations with North Vietnam at year's end (see below, pages 147–154). The "greatly improved" ARVN of 1972 had a variety of serious problems, the most obvious of which were continued poor leadership and a high desertion rate.

In my September 1974 survey, the American generals seemed to approve of the Vietnamization program but obviously felt that we waited until too late to begin it.

Was the Vietnamization program (efforts beginning in 1969) soundly conceived?   *Percentage*
   (1) Yes   58
   (2) Partially—but moved too fast   24
   (3) Partially—but moved too slow   9
   (4) No   6
   (5) No answer   3

Timing of Vietnamization
   (1) Program should have been emphasized years be-
      fore   73

(2) Program was conducted about the right time,
    considering all factors   19
(3) Program moved too fast   6
(4) Other or no answer   2

Another aspect of Vietnamization which was of basic importance to the success of the effort was pacification. By mid-1969, while the Vietnamization program was under way, the Thieu Government mounted a major effort to secure the rural areas. The effort had three central features: sustained local security; an intense effort to destroy the guerrilla infrastructure; and efforts at land reform and self-help projects for the villages.[7] There was also an attempt at village and hamlet elections that year; it had mixed success.

Evaluation of progress in this aspect of Vietnamization is harder than evaluating the improvement in the armed forces which we have previously discussed. For one thing there were more intangibles, and for another there were greater opportunities for deceptive reporting by American officials in Vietnam. Given the intense United States effort to "make it work," and the high level of interest, beginning at the White House, dishonest reporting was inevitable.

A disillusioned embassy official in Saigon, commenting on material being prepared for the Ambassador to present to President Nixon on pacification in the spring of 1969, had this to say privately: "The documents speak for themselves. The analysis has been considerably modified. The result is a totally misleading and unbelievably optimistic view of the local elections. This kind of dangerous diplomatic apologetics is what got us into Vietnam, and will one day make Vietnam an American tragedy. The genre of tragedy no bureaucrat or general will be able to disguise."

It was, of course, not just the Americans who were involved in telling Washington what it wanted to hear about pacification. Then Vice President Ky admitted to one United States official that Thieu's practice of ordering a province or district chief to achieve 90 or 98 percent pacification resulted in highly misleading figures. The local official, he pointed out, could by selective reporting always claim to have achieved the goal when in fact he had not.

There is an unclassified RAND paper on Vietnamization which was commissioned by Dr. Kissinger in his role as Presidential ad-

7. Lawrence E. Grinter, "South Vietnam's Pacification Denied," *Spectrum*, 3 (July 1975), p. 63.

viser. The paper was written by Guy J. Pauker and used 1970 as a data base.[8] In it the author confessed to a drastic change in outlook. From 1955 until 1969, this expert on Vietnam had not believed that the policies pursued by the United States in Vietnam could succeed. But now, early in 1970, he had come to realize that the great expenditures of American resources "may have accomplished a feat of political alchemy." He felt that government of South Vietnam could be viable if our aid continued and if we accepted some "low-level Communist violence." Bernard Brodie writes that the report was received with great satisfaction by both Nixon and Kissinger.[9] One can see why, since it confirmed what was coming through official channels and also what they wanted to hear.

How was pacification coming along? By mid-1970, when Vietnamization was well under way, United States and South Vietnamese efforts had actually pushed the Viet Cong out of areas they had controlled, to the point where they were in charge of less than 5 percent of the 12,000 hamlets in South Vietnam, although about 25 percent of the hamlets were contested. There were a number of reasons, including the quantity of United States resources available to government-controlled areas, and a drop in the popularity of the Viet Cong. People simply wanted the war to go away, so they could go back to work in their fields.

After the above is said, it should be added that most persons who knew realized that the gains were fragile and that the Viet Cong infrastructure remained intact, although it needed rebuilding. There was considerable uncertainty over the durability of the pacification achievements and the degree to which they could be sustained as the withdrawal of American forces accelerated.

By mid-1972 pacification had regressed considerably from its peak of two years earlier. The key event was the Communist Easter Offensive of 1972. For the first time in several years, the Communists were causing wide disruption in rural areas. Largely this resulted from the diversion of ARVN units from pacification programs to meet the North Vietnamese offensive. By the eve of the truce, the government had lost control of perhaps 20 percent of the population as a result of the Easter offensive. This was significant, for in certain areas the government's presence had completely disappeared. The Viet Cong could again recruit, tax, and

8. Guy J. Pauker, *An Essay on Vietnamization* (Santa Monica, California, Rand, 1971).

9. Brodie, *War and Politics*, p. 203.

propagandize in many areas formerly controlled by the Saigon government—and, it might be added, ones that the government still claimed to control. Base areas formerly closed to the VC were now available, as were infiltration routes formerly blocked. By the time of the Paris Accords in early 1973, the pacification part of Vietnamization was in a shaky and deteriorating condition.

The Easter Offensive of 1972

The North Vietnamese offensive that began on March 30, 1972, was in retrospect the major event of the war during the four-year period from the arrival of the Nixon Administration in January 1969 until the signing of the truce in January 1973. Before turning to a consideration of that offensive, we will look at the redeployment and state of United States forces during this period.

The last big battle of the war for these forces was the Cambodian incursion of May 1970 previously discussed. At that point American forces were down about 20 percent from their peak authorization of 549,500 in the spring of 1969. By May 1971 the authorized strength was down 50 percent from the peak, and by the time the Easter offensive was at its height in 1972, American forces were down 85 percent from their peak. [10]

During this long period of declining strength and gradual withdrawal from combat, there were serious morale problems and a deterioration in personnel quality, accompanied by dissent within the ranks, drug abuse, and racial tensions. In 1971 a series of news stories appeared on the sad state of American forces, the United States Army in particular. Allegedly, about one in ten soldiers was addicted to heroin. Fragging of unpopular officers was not uncom-

10. The general officer respondents to the survey seemed generally to approve of the manner in which the Army role was terminated, although there was a definite minority who thought termination could have been handled more rapidly.

Termination:	Percentage
1. Termination of U.S. Army role was handled about right	64
2. Army should have left faster and earlier	18
3. Army should have stayed in some sort of combat mode	8
4. Other or no answer	10

mon and there were many stories of refusals by small units and individual soldiers to engage in combat.

There is no question that as time went on, the deterioration in the expeditionary force increased to the point where by 1972 it was serving very little purpose except a political one—as a bargaining point in the on-going Paris negotiations. There were many reasons for this deterioration, chief among them being that the United States purpose in the war had become so unclear that no one wanted to be the last to die. There was also the problem of idleness. With three important exceptions, United States forces played no combat role in the Easter offensive. The exceptions were United States advisers with South Vietnamese ground units, American airpower, and American logistical support for the South Vietnamese defenders.

For several years beginning in mid-1969, the Viet Cong and North Vietnamese had maintained a fairly low profile during the process of Vietnamization. This approach was apparently based upon the conclusion that main-unit confrontations with U.S., ARVN, and allied forces were, for the moment, at least, losing propositions. Hence there was a return to protracted warfare involving small unit actions. This was set forth in July 1969 in the most comprehensive Viet Cong document ever obtained by American intelligence, labeled Resolution Number 9. The underlying assumption was apparently that American patience on the home front for continuing the effort had worn thin, and therefore the best policy was protracted warfare while the American forces were gradually withdrawn.

By 1972, however, the situation had changed. Events called for new decisions on the part of the North Vietnamese leadership, which led to an expansion of the conflict. There is still little definite evidence as to why the North Vietnamese opted for large-scale conventional warfare in the spring of 1972, but it seems that the decision was based on several considerations. First, from their point of view, Vietnamization seemed to be succeeding. If the picture was not as rosy as Nixon and Kissinger were hearing, some degree of success was nevertheless being achieved. Second, this was the time of Nixon's visit to China, and soon there would be the visit to Moscow which culminated in the SALT I agreements. Time was of the essence for North Vietnam, confronted with what seemed to be a rapprochement between the major powers of East and West. Finally, this was the year of an American presidential election, and was not the lesson of 1968 that an American administration was the most vulnerable during an election year?

We should make no mistake about it: Hanoi's 1972 effort was enormous. The resources channeled into the Easter offensive meant postponing needed economic development and required additional manpower from a society that had already sacrificed heavily during the long war. The offensive was not on the guerrilla pattern of Tet 1968, nor was the manpower to be sacrificed coming from the Viet Cong, as it had then. Rather, modern weapons such as tanks and self-propelled artillery were involved, as well as surface-to-air and anti-tank missiles. The manpower sacrificed this time would be North Vietnamese. All in all, it was a major gamble.

The operation against South Vietnam consisted of three thrusts, the chief one across the demilitarized zone in the north and the others in the II and III Corps areas further south. There was also some diversionary activity in the Delta.[11] Beginning on March 30, the initial thrust in the north, by the equivalent of four divisions, was successful. Hitting a fairly new and green ARVN division, the 3rd, the North Vietnamese forces rolled through the northern province of Quang Tri and its capital of the same name. Fighting surged back and forth, with some of the early ARVN actions ineptly executed and victimized by South Vietnamese bureaucratic politics. When the fabled General Truong was brought up from the Delta to command the I Corps, the Communist advance toward Hue was halted and then rolled back. Quang Tri city was captured in September, although the North Vietnamese retained control of large portions of the province. Fighting went on until October, when word came of the impending truce.

The major factor that influenced this battle and others to be mentioned below was the decision made by President Nixon to provide United States support at two levels. Strategically, he began an intensified bombing campaign against the North and mined its harbors. At the tactical level, the United States provided aerial fire support, including B-52's. Whatever their lack of effec-

11. At this writing (summer of 1976) I have not come across a full-scale work on the Easter Offensive. The most comprehensive article I have encountered was completed in the spring of 1973 and published the following year: A. P. Serong, "The 1972 Easter Offensive," *Southeast Asia Perspectives*, 10 (Summer 1974).

tiveness earlier, when the enemy was employing guerrilla tactics, there was no question of the effectiveness of American airpower against the conventional mode the North Vietnamese Army had now adopted. It had a vulnerable logistics tail: tanks and artillery need petrol and ammunition. Again, these large weapons systems were themselves vulnerable to air and ground weapons. One of the generals who responded to my questionnaire commented that the B-52's "were decisive in stopping the advance of the North Vietnamese toward Hue and permitted us to retake Quang Tri."

The assault against II Corps began on March 31, the day after the action was initiated in the north. The initial results were North Vietnamese successes, culminating in three months of horror for many of the occupants of the northern part of the coastal province of Binh Dinh and the capture by the NVA of Dak To in the highlands province of Kontum. Kontum city itself was surrounded, but again the B-52's took their toll and the ARVN held the city.

In the critical III Corps area, Loc Ninh—close to the Cambodian border—fell to the North Vietnamese a few days after they began their assault on April 2. Thereafter the battle raged farther south against the small provincial capital of An Loc. There was much television coverage of this action by American networks, the most memorable scene being one of a small child running from an action with napalm burning her clothing. With the help of the ARVN 21st Division from the Delta, An Loc, or what was left of it, held and Thieu himself was able to visit the town on July 7.

Actions in the Delta were diversionary—the most noteworthy being Thieu's boldness in moving a division from there to help in the siege of An Loc, and the steadfastness of the Popular Forces, who gave a good account of themselves in the absence of that division.

What did the campaign amount to for both sides and what were the lessons? For the North Vietnamese, the offensive cost them an estimated 50,000 to 75,000 dead. Some 700 of their tanks were destroyed in South Vietnam. Their logistics system, they learned, would have to be improved to field and keep up with a modern conventional army. Another lesson concerned the difficulty and perhaps the impossibility of employing conventional forces against American airpower without any airpower to counter. By 1975, when they overran South Vietnam, they had improved their logistics, and of course by then there was no American airpower: Congress, by amendment to an appropriations bill, had prohibited any American combat action after August 15, 1973, without the express approval of the Congress.

For South Vietnam, perhaps 30,000 had been killed. Their army had held, but American support and advisers had been critical. Also, a crippling blow to their position was the continued presence of North Vietnamese forces in South Vietnam. As it turned out, the truce signed several months after the end of the Easter offensive permitted the North Vietnamese to retain the territory they had gained during their offensive of 1972. Despite all their losses, therefore, the Hanoi leadership had again gained substantially from what might otherwise have been a military disaster. This time the gain was geographical, involving occupied territory, rather than psychological, as had been Tet 1968.

Final Agreements and Estimates

The Easter offensive had ground to a complete halt by October 1972, and it was evident in Paris that a truce was near. The talks had been going on sporadically since late in the Johnson Administration. In overall terms, the goals of the participating parties during the last year of the negotiations can be summed up as follows: The United States was looking for a graceful way out, which would leave the South Vietnamese with a reasonable chance for survival. The North Vietnamese leadership wanted an end to the destruction of their country by American air power, and an agreement that would set the stage for eventual unification of the two Vietnams. The Thieu government wanted South Vietnam to survive as an independent nation and the United States to remain a presence in that country as long as possible. The National Liberation front, or more correctly the Provisional Revolutionary Government, wanted to survive as a workable political force in South Vietnam.

In the course of negotiations, sometimes there were eight points being discussed, sometimes seven, sometimes nine. Whatever the number, the issues concerned troop withdrawal, cease-fire, prisoner release, political settlement, international guarantees, foreign intervention, and reparations. To include details of the talks would take volumes, but the final agreements can be put concisely.

Signed on January 27, 1973, in Paris, they include the following provisions:

(1) An in-place cease-fire on January 28, 1973.
(2) United States forces allowed sixty days to withdraw.
(3) Prisoners of war to be released.
(4) Establishment of an International Commission of Control and Supervision with a broad charter to handle disagreements between parties to the agreement.
(5) Provisions for general elections at a later date.

Although the terms of the agreement represented compromises on both sides, they were not equally acceptable to the North and South. Some advantages that the Saigon government had held during the war were altered by the treaty. The most obvious change to the detriment of Saigon was the final withdrawal of the United States military. Another major disadvantage to the Thieu government was that North Vietnamese forces were permitted to remain in South Vietnam. In effect, the parts of several southern provinces seized in the Easter offensive were retained by the North, and that would have considerable significance for the future. The agreement may have been the best the United States could get in the divided political climate at home, but it clearly was not very good from Thieu's point of view. As a sweetener, we later discovered, Nixon promised Thieu that United States military force would be reapplied in the event of gross violations of the agreement by the North. Perhaps in January 1973 Nixon thought this was possible. It clearly was not possible after the passage of the Case-Church amendment, which prohibited appropriation of funds for American combat forces in Vietnam after August 15, 1973.

The American military commander responsible for the final departure of United States combat forces was General Fred C. Weyand. Like his two predecessors in Vietnam, he, too, went on to become Army Chief of Staff. Unlike them, he was not a graduate of West Point, but held an A.B. degree in criminology from the University of California. Weyand did not have the combat background of Abrams or Westmoreland, but he was an extremely effective staff officer and commander. He has a charming personality and the ability to gain people's confidence. He was particularly good with the press on Vietnam until he stretched matters a bit far in the course of explaining the need for more aid to Saigon about a month before the regime fell in 1975 and while it was in full rout.

In any case, it was up to Weyand as the last COMUSMACV to make the final military estimate of the status of the South Vietnamese forces as the Americans departed. Vietnamization had, he believed, succeeded. However, the North Vietnamese forces in South Vietnam enjoyed a forward position, with relatively unrestricted ability to resupply and reinforce. In the event that Hanoi with external help attempted to pursue a military solution, the United States would be faced with a decision on reinvolvement. In other words, the South Vietnam government could not possibly make it alone against a major push by the North.

As for the future of the Republic of Vietnam's armed forces, their capabilities depended on Thieu's ability to overcome the deep corruption in the government which was weakening public confidence. The capability of the armed forces would also depend on their ability to overcome weaknesses in leadership, logistics, tactics, and troop morale. Finally and most important, Weyand felt, was the continuation of adequate military and other assistance from the United States.

In my September 1974 survey there was one question designed to obtain the generals' judgment on how well Vietnamization had succeeded with ARVN by that time. Their views of ARVN were not highly optimistic.

Success of Vietnamization by 1974:   *Percentage*
    (1) ARVN is a very acceptable fighting force   8
    (2) ARVN is adequate and chances of their holding in the
        future are better than fifty-fifty   57
    (3) It is doubtful ARVN will make it against a firm push
        in the future by VC/NVN forces   25
    (4) Other or no answer   10

I then asked a wrap-up question—whether it had all been worth the effort. In viewing the responses, it must be borne in mind that although September 1974 was only seven months from the final debacle, the situation in Vietnam did not appear as fragile as we now know it was.

Were the results of the war worth the effort, considering casualties, disruption of the United States

political scene, and side effects on United States
society and the United States military?   *Percentage*
  (1) Were worth the effort   14
  (2) Were worth the effort, but the effort should
      have been greater   25
  (3) Should not have progressed past an advisory effort   25
  (4) Were not worth the effort   28
  (5) Other or no answer   8

In effect, over 50 percent of the Army General officers who commanded in Vietnam thought, in September 1974, that the United States forces should not have participated in combat in Vietnam.

Afterward

In the early months after the Paris agreements, there was some minor maneuvering by both South and North forces to obtain more favorable cease-fire positions. In general, though, the initial main task for Hanoi was reconstructing its own economic base at home. The threat posed by North Vietnam forces, along with the political contest with the Viet Cong, kept South Vietnam fully mobilized.

As 1973 moved into 1974, it became evident that the North expected to remain permanently in the South. The Ho Chi Minh trail became an all-weather highway. In time, an oil pipeline appeared. Supplies and weapons were routinely shipped south, as were troop replacements and reinforcements.

The critical arena for South Vietnam became more and more the United States. Watergate in those years was taking its toll, and an increasingly assertive Congress showed less and less inclination to continue to support the South Vietnamese government. This can be illustrated by the following figures on military assistance support:

U.S. Military Assistance to South Vietnam
(billions of dollars)

	FY 73	*FY 74*	*FY 75*
Requested by DOD	$2.924	$1.185	$1.450
Appropriated by Congress	2.562	907	700
Amount cut by Congress	$ 362	$ 278	$ 750

What this meant in time was that more and more the armed forces of the South survived only by cannibalizing equipment, deferring maintenance, and becoming less and less able to counter an increasingly aggressive and probing enemy. Weaknesses showed themselves especially in the Vietnamese Air Force's operational capability and in ARVN's inability to adjust to the changing environment. ARVN had, of course, been trained in the American Army style of enormous outlays of ammunition—which were no longer available.

The readjustment was never made by ARVN, but attempts were. In April 1974 Thieu instructed the troops on ammunition conservation. He pointed out that the lavish days of American support were over and that "we must fight in a Vietnamese manner," which meant "defeating the enemy by determination rather than materials." Specifically he advised: "Use helicopters only in cases of absolute necessity; don't be tied to Air Force or Artillery support." Perhaps these instructions were sound, but after all those years of a different model, they were almost impossible to implement meaningfully.

Perhaps more important than the problems of materiel support were the problems of morale, which is the backbone of any armed force. The continued persistence of the North and its suppliers, the dwindling nature of United States support, and the realization that even American airpower would no longer be applied to gross violations of the truce were cumulatively too much, and in the end morale cracked.

There were other military problems that decreased the battle readiness of the South Vietnamese forces. In addition to their dependence on logistic assistance during the American period, the South Vietnamese had enjoyed enormous intelligence support from United States forces. Now without this support, they were unable to adjust to a new kind of battlefield in which enemy capabilities and location became, if not entirely unknown, at the least vague. The organization of the South Vietnamese armed forces was also a problem. This was especially true of the tendency of the Army and Air Force to go their own ways—a divisive force that became especially acute during the final battles in the spring of 1975.

There is one further factor that should be mentioned—Thieu himself. After the American departure in early 1973, he became increasingly rigid and exercised a very tight control on the armed forces. It automatically deprived the military leadership of any flexibility in decision-making and made for a highly politicized military force, both in management and in operations. The outcome was Thieu's precipitous order to abandon the Highlands and the wooden execution of that order by the Corps Commander, described above in Chapter 1.

As the American people watched the debacle on television in the spring of 1975, they were seeing an event that had many causes. Suffice it to conclude here that if it had not previously been evident enough, the final rout exposed Vietnamization for the fraud and deception that it was.

Conclusions

It remains to ask the question: what can we conclude from this reassessment of the Vietnam War, viewed principally from the perspective of its Army General Officer operational managers? I would like to set forth a brief interpretation of the data obtained from the responses to the September 1974 questionnaire,[1] and then, in a broader context, I shall offer insights of my own, based upon both the data of the questionnaire and my research into the war.

The Survey Responses and Hypotheses Reconsidered

Let us begin by considering the first three hypotheses (above, pages 11–12):

1. *Respondents will manifest some dissatisfaction with those aspects of the war which were under Washington's managerial control.*

2. *Respondents will be generally satisfied with those aspects of the war which were under the managerial control of the U.S. Army personnel at the theater level.*

3. *Respondents will express satisfaction with and pride in the professionalism of United States Army personnel.*

1. Those interested in a complete analysis should read Appendix II, below.

After examining the data, one finds considerable support for the three hypotheses proposed above. Predictably, respondents viewed Washington's management in a negative light; indeed, over 70 percent of those completing the questionnaire held negative views. At the same time, views of theater-level performance tended to be favorable, although somewhat less glowing than might be expected from respondents who had such a substantial career investment in the matter. Similarly, assessments of United States Army professionalism were positive, but again less than strikingly so.

Hypothesis 4 concerned ARVN and was stated as follows:

Respondents will be generally pessimistic with regard to the capabilities of ARVN to defend against Viet Cong and North Vietnamese forces.

The prediction is supported by the data presented earlier, specifically in the tables on pages 87 and 153. Respondents were notably unenthusiastic about the quality of ARVN general officer leadership, with nearly a third of the American generals expressing the view that their South Vietnamese counterparts were inadequate. Expectations concerning the eventual success of Vietnamization were only slightly more optimistic; fewer than 10 percent of the respondents regarded ARVN as better than adequate, and one in four expressed a lack of confidence in the ability of South Vietnamese forces to sustain a defense.

Hypothesis 5 concerned the news media:

Respondents will harbor negative views concerning coverage of the war by newspaper and television journalists.

Predictions of unfavorable attitudes toward the news media were strongly borne out, as the data in the tables on pages 132, 133 indicate. While the two questionnaire items are not strictly comparable, it is apparent that a majority of respondents viewed media coverage as irresponsible or disruptive of the war effort.

The sixth proposition stated:

Respondents will express some dissatisfaction with the overall results of the United States efforts.

The single question intended to elicit respondents' attitudes toward the overall outcome of the war (as viewed in September 1974, when the debacle of the following year was not expected) yielded findings that clearly confirm the above proposition. As the data indicate, 53 percent of the generals had in 1974 a negative retrospective assessment of the United States combat role in Southeast Asia.

Hypothesis 7—

Respondents will manifest a strong consensus in each of the substantive areas covered—

seemed reasonable and was based primarily on the homogeneity of the generals, as described in Chapter 1. However, one of the noteworthy patterns visible in the data presented throughout the book is the striking absence of consensus in all areas save that concerning the media and, to a lesser extent, the capabilities of ARVN. In addition to the magnitudes of the standard deviations shown below, page 178, the frequency distribution in the table on page 154 suggests that very strong differences of opinion exist among the respondents—differences that are more significant in the light of the homogeneity of the generals. The task of explaining the variation in supportive orientation was inhibited by this homogeneity and by the absence of data reflecting their ideological inclinations.

However, when the indices of orientations toward national-level management, theater-level management, and United States Army professionalism were combined additively to form an overall index of support, further tests revealed the influence of three independent variables. In general, graduates of West Point, members of the Infantry, and those with Airborne qualifications attained higher support scores than did their counterparts. In order to discern the relative influence of these variables, an analysis was conducted to assess the effect of each variable. Airborne qualification emerged as the most significant predictor of positive support.

The concept of a military mind may be attractive in a simplistic way, but it is evident from the wide variety of responses by the elite of the American Army of the Vietnam War that in this case the notion is not supported by empirical evidence. One thing that the responses show is a substantial degree of introspective criticism of the Army's own efforts. The point is interesting in view of the defensiveness alleged to be characteristic of military elites. There exist two plausible but untested interpretations of these inclinations toward self-criticism. In the first place, retrospective assessments of the war made in 1974 were formulated at a point when emotional aspects of the war and the exigencies of personnel responsibility had been largely attenuated, and the respondents were able to view their experience from a detached and presumably less idealized perspective. Secondly, critical inclinations were enabled to emerge in part because of the anonymous nature of the responses. This latter point raises the question why some of this group did not speak out earlier during the course of the war on such matters as the body count or on larger issues concerning the manner in which the war was being fought. Perhaps the main lesson for the future is that the system will have to permit more dissent without exacting the sacrifice of careers as the price.

Broader Considerations and Implications

The dissatisfaction of the operational managers of the war toward Washington-level (meaning civilian) management of the war should come as no surprise. It emerged strongly from the data previously presented and it is the major theme in the memoirs of General Westmoreland, who wrote: "However desirable the American system of civilian control of the military, it was a mistake to permit appointive civilian officials lacking military experience and knowledge of military history and oblivious to the lessons of Communist diplomatic machinations to wield undue influence in the decision-making process."[2] The main thesis of this argument is that the incremental application of power in Vietnam and the constraints placed on the use of power were the product of poor civilian decision-making. Furthermore, it is held that that approach led to a "no win" situation by permitting a vastly smaller country to marshal its resources in what it perceived to be a total war, and to extend the conflict until the patience of the American people was exhausted.

We shall never know what the result of a different strategy

2. William C. Westmoreland, *A Soldier Reports* (New York, Doubleday, 1976), p. 121.

would have been. We do know that graduated response did not work. Whatever else might be said about the approach taken, it did prevent the war from escalating beyond Indo-China, with all that the possibility of such a conflict conjures up. The main purpose here, however, is not to refight the war but to emphasize that one of the important themes that has developed from this study is that there was a major gap in civilian-military communications during the Vietnam War.

There is another aspect to civilian control than the one perceived by Westmoreland and some of his generals: civilians at all levels did not pay enough attention to what the military were doing in Vietnam. There is a long-standing tradition of autonomy for American commanders during time of war. From June 1965 onward, as we have described above (pages 34–46), Westmoreland was in a position to pursue operations within Vietnam pretty much as he wished. The Joint Chiefs were advocates for Westmoreland in Washington as he proceeded with his search and destroy, security, and pacification missions. In time, McNamara became disenchanted with the military approach in Vietnam, but he was reluctant to pay the price of speaking out against the strategy of the ground commander.

There was no special organizational machinery set up in Washington to manage the War.[3] Perhaps Secretary Laird's Vietnam Task Force which helped to manage Vietnamization in the Pentagon could be called a special organization. It came late, however, and was not especially important except as a coordinating device. The lack of an effective organization permitted the military to present a united front to the civilian leadership. As a result, Westmoreland's autonomy in running the war was fairly complete. Moreover, lack of any strategic guidance from Washington could also be interpreted by him as approval of the manner in which he was conducting the war.

One of the side problems that this autonomy generated was what turned to be the key variable: American public opinion simply was not considered by those who were actually planning how the war in the South was fought. This omission had obvious and significant implications, summed up in an extract from a 1969 speech by the British journalist Henry Brandon:

3. Chester Cooper attributes this to the notion, at least until 1967, that the war would not be a long one. Cooper, *The Lost Crusade* (New York, Dodd, Mead, 1970), pp. 424–425.

Before leaving Saigon on one of my periodic visits to Vietnam late in 1967, I asked the leading civilians and military in charge whether a reduction in the intensity of the war, a reduction of the cost in men and material, would not be worth striving for. I thought it might help to induce a more patient and forbearing attitude towards the war on the part of the American public. . . . Not surprisingly, they all reacted alike. They said it was not their business to include American domestic opinion in their calculations; that was up to President Johnson.[4]

There is another facet to the civilian-military relationship, in addition to the autonomy of the field commander, which is pertinent to this discussion. There has been a long-standing tradition of an adversary relationship between American civilian and military leadership, which was continued during the Indochinese War. We are not dealing here with whether the civilians were ultimately in charge. They were. The question is one of communication.

There are, it seems to me, two reasons for this relationship, which can be further defined as one of caution and bargaining. In the first place, the power bases of the two groups are different. The civilians—at least, the appointive and elected ones—have to keep in mind issues of an immediate nature bearing on domestic policy. The military, on the other hand, represent an entrenched bureaucracy who must live with the decisions, once made, while they watch the civilians come and go—civilians who do not always have to live with their own decisions.

Another facet is that the respective spheres of activity of the two adversaries tend to set up a systemic relationship. This is best illustrated in the budgetary process, especially in times of perceived shortfalls in the defense budget. Even a President as sure of himself in defense matters as Eisenhower had to struggle for eight years to keep the defense budget where he thought it should be. Meanwhile, he and his civilian policy-makers faced a recalcitrant group of Pentagon generals who felt defense was being shortchanged. Not all Presidents are as capable of dealing with the Pentagon as was Eisenhower.

Whatever the reasons for the adversarial relationship, let's accept it as being there, and consider the implications in terms of the Vietnam War. The war quite understandably caused the adversary

4. Quoted in Brodie, *War and Politics*, p. 439.

relationship to be minimized, as compared, say, with a peacetime budget struggle. The manner in which it was minimized, however, was to paper over the real issues of the war rather than to face up to them. Hence the preoccupation of the civilian leaders in Washington was with the concrete issues raised in Chapter 3: issues such as how large an increase in the size of the expeditionary force there should be, or how soon such an increase could be accomplished. The big questions about objectives or strategy were not debated until after the Tet 1968 Offensive.

Thus when Westmoreland writes that there were too many constraints imposed by civilians on his conduct of the war, he may be correct in one sense. From a different perspective, however, one can draw another conclusion: there was not *enough* civilian participation in terms of asking the big questions about what we were really doing in Vietnam.[5] In part, this was a matter of personality; I find it very difficult to believe that Dwight Eisenhower would ever have permitted himself to field an expeditionary force of a half million men in Vietnam. In part, it was also the "big war" mentality—let the military run it—in what was a very political affair indeed. Most of all, it was a lack of communication between civilians and military.

There is no pat solution to the problem, but a closer working rapport between the senior military and the President such as has not been maintained for years would certainly help. After all, by law the Joint Chiefs are the principal military advisers to the President. Of course, they work also for the Secretary of Defense, but what they do is too important for the Secretary to serve as a go-between on major matters. Both civilian and military should participate meaningfully with the President when he is making major decisions, and we must assume that in the future both sides would speak up if they had misgivings.

In addition to the military-civilian communications gap, it seems evident from the questionnaire data that considerable difference of opinion concerning the manner in which the war was fought existed among its general officer operational managers. As noted in the table on page 178, almost 31 percent of the generals had a negative outlook toward theater-level management of the war. More important are specific areas in which they had misgivings,

5. A well-known exception was George Ball, who assumed the role of "house objector" to the war. He was tolerated but did not exert great influence on the decision-making process.

such as search and destroy operations. Furthermore, when 61 percent of the Army generals who commanded in Vietnam say that the body count (the basis of measuring progress in a war of attrition) was often inflated, one is tempted to ask again, why did not these generals speak out at the time? The most frequent explanation is that their careers were at stake and they could not afford to make waves. Maureen Mylander, among others, believes that it is necessary to keep dissent private if one is to advance upward in rank.[6]

The failure to speak out during the Vietnam War concerning its conduct and the need to provide mechanisms for dissent within the system were publicly addressed by Vice Admiral William P. Mack at his retirement ceremony at Annapolis in the summer of 1975. It does seem clear that heeding public or even internal criticism of policy was not an established practice during the Vietnam War.

This is a difficult problem in any bureaucracy and especially in the military, with its traditional deference to rank and the requirements to conform. If any change is to be instituted, a start would be to eliminate the "can do" ethos. Everything just can't be done simply because a superior orders it. "Can do" has a place at some levels, perhaps, but it cannot cover all situations. It is tougher to oppose a policy than to say "Yes, sir" and pretend to make it work, but surely the American officer corps has the integrity to stand up and be counted. Fortunately, the present military leadership recognizes the problem; in this regard at least we can be hopeful, while retaining some skepticism, that there will be no more Vietnams.[7]

If there were wide areas of disagreement among the Army generals of the Vietnam War, there were two areas of consensus—on the Army of Vietnam, and on the role of the media in the war. The consensus in both cases was negative.

6. Maureen Mylander, *The Generals* (New York, Dial, 1974), pp. 210, 211. A more explicit critique along the same lines is in Edward L. King, *The Death of the Army* (New York, Saturday Review Press, 1972), pp. 106–108.

7. The problem of excessive careerism at the expense of integrity and other traditional values in the context of Vietnam was clearly recognized in the Army War College study previously mentioned, which was prepared for Army Chief of Staff Westmoreland in 1970. A number of corrective programs were instituted as a result. It is a bit early at this writing (1976) to know the long-range results of these programs.

In reacting negatively to the ARVN, the United States Army generals were admitting that our advisory effort in Vietnam was a failure. Former Prime Minister Ky of South Vietnam called it "a lamentable disaster that contributed largely to the eventual debacle in Vietnam . . . a gigantic con trick foisted on American public opinion."[8] Whether that is too harsh a criticism is difficult to say, in view of the outcome in 1975. When we view the effort as a whole, however, there are some conclusions to be drawn that could have applicability in other situations. One concerns the government of other indigenous allies whom we might consider helping. No matter how generous our military support and assistance, a country that is not politically cohesive and lacks legitimacy cannot achieve stability. There must be strong political and bureaucratic institutions to work with. We cannot significantly alter the nature of a society or its regime merely by volunteering our support.

Even though we assume for the moment that the South Vietnamese Government was perceived to be potentially viable, there was a major error in the manner in which we proffered advice and support. Too much effort was expended by advisers on getting along with the officials they were advising rather than on getting the job done. The result was a tendency to accept inadequate performance in order to maintain support. Pressure through the reduction of support needs to be applied where performance is inadequate. This does not mean taking charge; quite the opposite: the results must come about through indigenous efforts. Robert Komer, who knows as much about this problem as anyone, has put it this way: "When the U.S. is supporting local programs, it should not hesitate where necessary to use the leverage provided by this support."[9]

Finally, any advisory effort on our part should be tailored to the specific culture and environment in question. We have earlier discussed the cultural differences between Americans and Vietnamese. What was possibly not recognized in time was the difference between the Vietnamese and Koreans. A certain approach still fresh in our minds had worked in Korea, and were Korea and Vietnam not both Asian countries? Actually, not only were the two Asian cultures different, but so also was the nature of the two wars,

8. Nguyen Cao Ky, *Twenty Years and Twenty Days* (New York, Stein and Day, 1976), p. 125.
9. R. W. Komer, *Bureaucracy Does Its Thing* (Santa Monica, California, Rand, 1972), p. 159.

at least until the final weeks in Vietnam. The Korean War was conventional, not guerrilla, and lasted a comparatively short time. For whatever reasons, the South Korean government was powerful to an extent that the GVN never really was, and accepted the notion that its forces would be under American command—something South Vietnam would never do. In sum, the Korean advisory model was applied in an alien situation and did not work.[10]

The only other area of consensus on the part of the Army generals was a negative reaction to the media, and that is quite a different story. One of the main themes running through General Westmoreland's memoirs is the adverse effect of the media not only on the public but on government officials. "Press and television," he wrote, "had created an aura not of victory but of defeat, which, coupled with the vocal anti-war elements, profoundly influenced timid officials in Washington."[11]

It does seem that the night-after-night television coverage of the war, with all its blood and killing beamed to homes throughout America, was a major factor in eroding public support for United States efforts in Vietnam. Few understood in advance what the impact on the public of the first televised war would be. Now that we know, what can be done about it in the future? Censorship is no answer. Media coverage, television and press, with its ability to influence the public sometimes fairly, sometimes unfairly, must be recognized as a given.

Obviously, future decisions to commit American forces to a combat situation must take into account the need to sustain public support in the face of an adversary media. The situation itself must be one in which American interests are clearly at stake in a way that can be made understandable to the public. An important element is the estimated duration of the conflict. American public support cannot be sustained throughout a long, inconclusive war.

An important corollary is the need for truthfulness in dealing with the public. From the president all the way to the field units, the practice of letting the facts speak for themselves is the best

10. The other side of the coin, developed above, pages 63–67, is to know the enemy as well as the ally. The Pentagon Papers indicate that the CIA alone had a sense of the determination and motivation of the North Vietnamese. This knowledge seems not to have been absorbed by the remainder of the bureaucracy until late in the war.

11. Westmoreland, p. 410.

hope. In the Vietnam War there was too much tricky optimism from LBJ on down. Furthermore, there was too much concealing of the implications of half-announced decisions. Certainly the media have their own lessons to learn from Vietnam, but so does the government, including the military.

As these lines are being written in the summer of 1976, the collapse of South Vietnam is a year behind us. There is no great debate about the lost war, about what went wrong, but the dead hand of that misadventure is present in domestic and foreign matters. For one thing there is an understandable caution about foreign commitments, especially where these might involve military forces. Another reaction, at least partially attributable to the war, is a disillusionment with détente, along with congressional and public support for increased defense spending for the first time in many years—the latter perhaps in the hope of reestablishing American credibility after the Vietnam debacle.

Vietnam clearly established the limits of American power, but its excesses and confused strategy cannot be used indefinitely as a rationale to avoid future challenges that we are going to face as a global power. The Vietnam War lies lurking in the background, not yet clearly understood and perhaps being misread. It is not going to go away. It may, as President Ford said, be "behind us" in one respect, but in others it will be with us for a decade, perhaps for a generation.

It needs to be looked at objectively and unemotionally. General William Westmoreland, whose name will always be linked with it, put it well early in 1976:

> There should be no witch hunt over Vietnam, but before we close off debate, we should remember that whatever the mistakes, we were in Vietnam for serious and moral purposes, and we should have no fear of introspective analysis. Policy makers, planners, bureaucrats, newsmen—all must search to discern these mistakes and to heed the lessons of Vietnam so that in the end the bitter experience we have undergone can help us to become a better and stronger nation.[12]

If this book makes even a small contribution to that debate, it will more than have repaid my efforts.

12. Ibid., p. 423.

Appendix I

Questionnaire for Selected United States Army General Officers (September 1974)

There are ten areas of questions shown below. It is recognized that not all respondents will be equally at home on all areas. However, as a key member of the United States Army in the Vietnamese War your opinions will be valuable in all areas. If you think a question does not have the preferred option write in one you like and answer it. Place "X's" in the boxes that correspond to the answer you select. All questions, with the exception of "4D," are as you now view these matters. You may, of course, have viewed them differently in the past. If there is any question about which you have no view or knowledge please make a marginal notation to that effect.

1. **Objectives of War: Understanding and Validity**   *Percentage*

   A. Were United States objectives in Vietnam prior to
      Vietnamization (1969)
      (1) Clear and understandable   29
      (2) Not as clear as they might have been   33
      (3) Rather fuzzy—needed rethinking as war progressed   35
      (4) Other or no answer   3

   B. Did lower echelons understand those objectives?
      (1) Seemed to understand   20
      (2) Understood imperfectly   57
      (3) Not important—understanding important for them
          was day-to-day issues   20
      (4) Other or no answer   3

   C. Did you feel that United States objectives prior to
      Vietnamization (1969) were
      (1) Capable of achievement   43
      (2) Not capable of achievement   19
      (3) By 1968 not capable of achievement—should have
          been revised   25
      (4) Always should have been more limited   8
      (5) Other or no answer   5

2. **Were the Tactics, Forces, and Their Employment**
    Properly Conceived and Executed?   *Percentage*

    A. Was the search and destroy concept
        (1) Sound   38
        (2) Sound when first implemented—not later   26
        (3) Not sound   32
        (4) Other or no answer   4

    B. Execution of search and destroy tactics was
        (1) Superior   7
        (2) Adequate   35
        (3) Left something to be desired   51
        (4) Other or no answer   7

    C. Was close air support
        (1) About right quantitatively   64
        (2) Not enough quantitatively   6
        (3) Too much considering the nature of the war   28
        (4) Other or no answer   2

    D. Was artillery support
        (1) About right   57
        (2) Not enough   10
        (3) Too much considering the nature of the war   30
        (4) Other or no answer   3

    E. B-52 strikes in South Vietnam were
        (1) Very valuable   47
        (2) Useful but not vital   36
        (3) Not worth the effort   15
        (4) Other or no answer   2

    F. How do you feel about the large scale operations
        (Attleboro, Cedar Falls, etc.)?
        (1) Use early in war correct   28
        (2) Should have been continued   21
        (3) Overdone from the beginning   42
        (4) Other or no answer   9

    G. Were herbicides as used in Vietnam
        (1) Necessary when used, and controls imposed were
            about correct   53
        (2) More controls should have been imposed   20
        (3) Not worth their value considering physical
            damage they caused   21
        (4) Other or no answer   6

H. Use of Rome plows was
   (1) About right, and they were properly controlled   43
   (2) There should have been more Rome plow companies   37
   (3) A questionable program except in some select areas,
       considering physical side effects   16
   (4) Other or no answer   4

I. Was CS gas
   (1) A necessary assist for small units which should not
       have been given up for any reason   63
   (2) Could have been given up for larger political objectives
       such as overall restrictions on chemical warfare   29
   (3) Other or no answer   8

J. Command and control was
   (1) About right   57
   (2) Should have been more central control—too many
       units going their own way   3
   (3) There was overcontrol of units by higher commanders   35
   (4) Other or no answer   5

K. Interservice cooperation with Air Force
   (1) Outstanding   60
   (2) Adequate but could be improved   37
   (3) Not satisfactory, big improvement needed   2
   (4) Other or no answer   1

L. Interservice cooperation with Marines
   (1) Outstanding   22
   (2) Adequate but could be improved   43
   (3) Not satisfactory, big improvement needed   17
   (4) Other or no answer   18

M. Interservice cooperation with Navy
   (1) Outstanding   29
   (2) Adequate but could be improved   45
   (3) Not satisfactory, big improvement needed   13
   (4) Other or no answer   13

N. Capability of the VC prior to Tet 68
   (1) Skilled and tough fighters   57
   (2) Adequate fighters   33
   (3) Left something to be desired as fighters   6
   (4) No answer   4

O. Capability of Army of NVN
   (1) A skilled and tough force   44

(2) An adequate force   32
(3) A force that left something to be desired   23
(4) Other   1

3. **Were the Results of the War Measured Properly?**   *Percentage*

A. The measurement of progress system with all its indicators
    (1) Was a valid system to measure progress in the war   2
    (2) Valid to a point but should have been used more as a
        management tool rather than to measure progress   62
    (3) Not a valid way to measure progress in the war   32
    (4) Other or no answer   4

B. One important indicator was kill ratio. Was this
    (1) A valuable indicator and necessary in managing the war   4
    (2) A rough device that was better than others   35
    (3) A misleading device to estimate progress   55
    (4) Other or no answer   6

C. The kill ratio was based upon body count. Was body count
    (1) Within reason accurate   26
    (2) Underestimated even considering the amount added by
        MACV to account for later deaths of wounded, etc.   3
    (3) Often inflated   61
    (4) Other or no answer   10

D. Prior to 1968 the will and determination of the enemy
    to continue the war
    (1) Was taken into account   20
    (2) Was considered, but data were insufficient   19
    (3) Was not sufficiently considered   56
    (4) Other or no answer   5

4. **Efforts to Improve ARVN**   *Percentage*

A. Was the Vietnamization program (efforts beginning in
    1969) soundly conceived?
    (1) Yes   58
    (2) Partially—but moved too fast   24
    (3) Partially—but moved too slow   9
    (4) No   6
    (5) No answer   3

B. Timing of Vietnamization
    (1) Program should have been emphasized years before   73
    (2) Program was conducted about the right time consider-
        ing all factors   19

      (3) Program moved too fast   2
      (4) Other or no answer   6

C. Success of Vietnamization by 1974
    (1) ARVN is a very acceptable fighting force   8
    (2) ARVN is adequate and chances of their holding in the
        future are better than fifty-fifty   57
    (3) It is doubtful ARVN will make it against a firm push
        in the future by VC/NVN forces   25
    (4) Other or no answer   10

D. ARVN general officer leadership as you viewed it when
you were in Vietnam was
    (1) Quite strong   6
    (2) As good as could be expected—fair to good   57
    (3) Inadequate   32
    (4) Other or no answer   5

5. The Pacification Program   *Percentage*

A. Administration
    (1) Should have been completely administered by United
        States military   17
    (2) The CORDS arrangement under a military field force
        commander or equivalent was the optimum
        arrangement   26
    (3) More should have been done by the Vietnamese 44
    (4) Other or no answer   13

B. The hamlet evaluation system (as modified) was
    (1) A good way to measure progress in pacification 2
    (2) Had weaknesses but was about as good as could have
        been devised   75
    (3) Not a valid way to measure progress in pacification 19
    (4) No answer   4

6. Professionalism of United States Army Officer Corps *Percentage*

A. Middle ranks (Col., Lt. Col.)
    (1) Highly professional   70
    (2) Fairly professional   26
    (3) Left a good deal to be desired   2
    (4) No answer   2

B. Lower ranks (Maj., Capt., Lt.)
    (1) Considering age, highly professional   62
    (2) Fairly professional   31

      (3) Left a good deal to be desired   6
      (4) No answer   1

C. Junior officer leadership (Capt., Lt.)
    (1) Improved throughout the war   34
    (2) Remained about the same throughout the war   30
    (3) Deteriorated as the war went on   32
    (4) Other or no answer   4

D. Compared to the Korean War or World War II, United States Army Officers were

	WW II	Korean War
(1) More professional	43	33
(2) About the same	35	47
(3) Less professional	12	10
(4) Other or no answer	10	10

E. Careerism (i.e. ticket punching, rapid rotation in jobs, etc.) was
    (1) No problem   9
    (2) Somewhat of a problem   50
    (3) A serious problem   37
    (4) No answer   4

F. Greatest strength of officer corps was
    (1) Technical competence   24
    (2) Tactical competence   7
    (3) Leadership ability   59
    (4) Other or no answer   10

G. The Non-Commissioned Officer Corps in Vietnam was
    (1) Highly competent   25
    (2) Adequate   52
    (3) Left something to be desired   20
    (4) Other or no answer   3

7. **Rules of Engagement**   *Percentage*

A. Before My Lai the rules of engagement were
    (1) Well understood throughout the chain of command   29
    (2) Fairly well understood throughout the chain of command   49
    (3) Frequently misunderstood throughout the chain of command   17
    (4) Other or no answer   5

B. Before My Lai became public knowledge, the rules of
   engagement were
   (1) Carefully adhered to throughout the chain of command   19
   (2) Fairly well adhered to throughout the chain of
       command   61
   (3) Not particularly considered in the day-to-day conduct
       of the war   15
   (4) Other or no answer   5

8. **Role of the Media**   *Percentage*

   A. Newspaper coverage of the war was
      (1) Generally responsible and played an important role in
          keeping United Stated informed (a few exceptions)   8
      (2) Uneven. Some good but many irresponsible   51
      (3) On the whole tended to be irresponsible and disruptive
          to United States efforts in Vietnam   38
      (4) Other or no answer   3
   B. Television coverage of the war
      (1) Good for American people to see actual scenes of
          fighting about when they occurred   4
      (2) Probably not a good thing in balance because such
          coverage tends to be out of context   39
      (3) Not a good thing since there was a tendency to go for
          the sensational, which was counterproductive to the
          war effort   52
      (4) Other or no answer   5

9. **Was the Outcome of the War Satisfactory?**   *Percentage*

   A. Termination
      (1) Termination of United States Army role was handled
          about right   64
      (2) Army should have left faster and earlier   18
      (3) Army should have stayed in some sort of combat mode   8
      (4) Other or no answer   10
   B. Were the results of the war worth the effort considering
      casualties, disruption of the United States political scene,
      and side effects on United States society and the United
      States military?
      (1) Were worth the effort   14
      (2) Were worth the effort, but the effort should have been
          greater   25
      (3) Should not have progressed past an advisory effort   25
      (4) Were not worth the effort   28
      (5) Other or no answer   8

10. If We Had to Do It Over—In What Areas Would You Recommend the Greatest Changes? (Any number or combination may be answered yes)   *Percentage*

A. Defining the objectives   91

B. Changing the tactics   62

C. Measuring the results   56

D. Terminating the war   59

    IF YES   Earlier termination   46
               OR
               Later termination   10
               Other   3

E. Improving the ARVN   91

    IF YES   Begin earlier   56
               OR
               Change the advisory system   3
               Both   32

F. Pacification program   81

    IF YES   Greater effort   35
               OR
               Administer differently   27
               Both   17
               No answer   2

G. Improve professionalism of officier corps

		Yes	No	No. Ans.
If yes	In tactical units	23	74	3
"X" all	In advisory units	35	62	3
that	At higher ranks	17	81	3
apply	At lower ranks	27	70	3
	Throughout	36	61	3

H. Reserve components   91   7   2

If yes	Mobilize earlier	26
"X" all	Mobilize more than token called up	26
that	Both	33
apply	Not mobilize at all	6

Appendix II

The Framework for the Hypotheses

Let us begin by considering the first three hypotheses, which were stated above in Chapters 1 and 7 as follows:

Respondents will manifest some dissatisfaction with those aspects of the war which were under Washington's managerial control.

Respondents will be generally satisfied with those aspects of the war which were under the managerial control of the U.S. Army personnel at the theater level.

Respondents will express satisfaction with and pride in the professionalism of U.S. Army personnel.

Composite indices designed to measure the respondents' orientations toward Washington-level management, theater-level management, and the overall professionalism of the United States Army were constructed and standardized as follows: For each of these concepts, relevant questionnaire responses were coded to reflect a positive, neutral, or negative orientation. The index of national-level management was constructed from eight items. Three of these concerned the clarity of United States objectives prior to 1969, their realism, and the desirability of redefining them; two dealt with the soundness and timing of the Vietnamization program; two others concerned the timing and management of the termination of the United States Army role in Vietnam; and a final item focused on the timing and extent of the mobilization of the Reserves.

The index of theater-level management was constructed from fourteen items. Eight sought to assess the respondents' orientations toward the soundness or efficacy of the following tactical issues: search and destroy operations; close air support; artillery support; B-52 strikes in South Vietnam; large-scale operations; herbicides; Rome plows; and CS gas. One item dealt with the value of the kill ratio as a measure of progress, and another with the validity of the body count. Two others dealt with the understanding of and adherence to the rules of engagement before My Lai. One item concerned the desirability of a change in tactics, while another concerned command and control.

The index of United States Army professionalism was comprised of seven items. Three concerned professionalism at the following levels: Colonel and Lieutenant Colonel; Major, Captain, and Lieutenant; and Non-Commissioned Officers. Two items sought a comparison of the professionalism of United States Army officers in Vietnam with that of their counterparts in World War II and Korea. One item concerned changes in the quality of junior officer leadership over the course of the war, while a final question dealt with problems of careerism. Components of a given measure were then combined additively, and each index was then transformed so that its possible values ranged from −10 to +10.

As Table 1 indicates, considerable support exists for the three hypotheses proposed above. Predictably, respondents viewed Washington's management in a generally negative light; indeed, over 70 percent of those completing the questionnaire failed to achieve neutral or positive scores on this index. At the same time, views of theater level performance tended to be favorable, although somewhat less glowing than might have been expected from respondents who had so substantial a career investment in the matter. Similarly, assessments of United States Army professionalism were positive, but again less than strikingly so.

Table 1
U.S. Army General Officers' Orientation Toward Management of Vietnam War and Professionalism of U.S. Army

	National Level Management	Theater Level Management	Professionalism
Mean	−2.76	1.15	1.93
Median	−2.69	1.46	2.38
Percentage unfavorable (scores below zero)	71.3	30.6	23.1
Standard deviation	3.65	4.16	3.29

Hypothesis 4 concerned ARVN: *Respondents will be generally pessimistic with regard to the capabilities of ARVN to defend against Viet Cong and North Vietnamese forces.*

The prediction that respondents would be pessimistic in their view of ARVN and its capabilities is supported by the data presented earlier, specifically in the tables on pages 87 and 153. Respondents were notably unenthusiastic about the quality of ARVN general officer leadership, with nearly a third of the American generals expressing the view that their

South Vietnamese counterparts were inadequate. Expectations concerning the eventual success of Vietnamization were only slightly more optimistic; fewer than 10 percent of the respondents regarded ARVN as better than adequate, while one in four expressed a lack of confidence in the ability of South Vietnamese forces to sustain a defense.

Hypothesis 5 concerned the news media: *Respondents will harbor negative views concerning coverage of the war by newspaper and television journalists.* Predictions of unfavorable attitudes toward the news media were strongly borne out, as the data in the tables on pages 132, 133 indicate. While the two questionnaire items are not strictly comparable, it is apparent that a majority of respondents viewed media coverage as irresponsible or disruptive of the war effort.

The sixth proposition stated that *respondents will express some dissatisfaction with the overall results of the U.S. efforts.* On page 154 a single question intended to elicit respondents' attitudes toward the overall outcome of the war (as viewed in September 1974, when the debacle of the following year was not expected) yielded findings that clearly confirm the above proposition. As the data on page 154 indicate, 53 percent of the generals can be characterized as having had in 1974 a negative retrospective assessment of the United States combat role in Southeast Asia.

Hypothesis 7, to the effect that *respondents will manifest a strong consensus in each of the substantive areas covered,* seemed reasonable and was based primarily on the homogeneity of the generals, as described in Chapter 1. One of the noteworthy patterns visible in the data presented throughout the book, however, is the striking absence of consensus in all areas save those of the media and, to a lesser extent, the capabilities of ARVN. In addition to the magnitudes of the standard deviations presented in the table on page 178, the frequency distribution in the table on page 154 suggests that some very strong differences of opinion exist among respondents—differences that are lent even more significance by the very homogeneity of the generals.

Another interesting finding is the apparent unidimensionality of response pattern. The correlation coefficients presented in Table 2 suggest the salience of a general supportive/critical distinction which transcends conceptual boundaries within the instrument. In other words, while the generals as a group may have regarded theater-level management more favorably than they did management from Washington, an individual with positive orientations in one response area tended to manifest them in others as well, with the exception of media coverage, where there was an overwhelming consensus in a negative direction.

The task of explaining the variation in supportive orientation was inhibited by the homogeneity of the respondents and by the absence of data reflecting their ideological inclinations.

Employing multiple regression, analysis of variance, cross-tabulation,

Table 2

Intercorrelations of Management and Professionalism Indices (Pearson's r)

	National Level Management	Theater Level Management	Professionalism
National level management		.47**	.32**
Theater level			.28*

$$n = 108$$
$$** \; p < .001$$
$$* \; p < .01$$

and bivariate correlation techniques, I sought to assess the influence of a number of plausible determinants of the variation in scores on the aforementioned indices, both singly and in additive combination. Although such variables as age, rank, length of army service, active/retired status, previous combat experience, and number, duration, and years of Vietnam combat tours were tested, no striking patterns emerged. There exists a weak negative relationship ($r = -.23$, $p = .05$) between the year the respondent last served in Vietnam and his score on the professionalism index. In other words, generals serving during the latter period of the war tended to be more critical of United States Army professionalism. Such a relationship tends to converge with conventional perceptions of deteriorating professionalism within lower ranks during the latter stages of the war.

When the indices of orientations toward national-level management, theater-level management, and United States Army professionalism were combined additively to form an overall index of support,[1] further tests revealed the influence of three independent variables. In general, graduates of West Point, members of the Infantry, and those with Airborne qualifications attained higher support scores than did their counterparts, as shown by the data in Table 3.

To discern the relative influence of these variables and the possibility of their combining interactively, a two-way analysis of variance was performed on each of the three possible two-variable combinations. In this manner it was possible to assess the main effect of each variable controlling sequentially for its plausible rivals, and to assess the interactive effect of each two-variable combination. The results of these analyses are shown below. Airborne qualification emerged as the only statistically significant predictor of positive support, and the amount of variance explained remained low. There were, moreover, no significant interactive influences.

1. Scores on this overall index ranged from -24 to $+20$; the median score was 1.43, and 42.6 percent of the respondents failed to register a neutral or positive score.

Table 3
Index of Overall Support for United States Effort in Vietnam

	Mean	Standard Deviation	N
Total sample	.322	8.42	(108)
USMA	1.147	8.39	(51)
non-USMA	−.415	8.46	(57)
Infantry	1.304	8.57	(67)
Artillery	−1.218	8.43	(23)
Armor	−1.362	7.70	(18)
Airborne	2.226	8.06	(55)
			$E^2 = .08$
non-Airborne	−1.653	8.41	(53)

While non-West Point, non-Airborne, non-Infantry generals were most critical of the war, their negative orientation was not greater than an additive model would predict.

These findings were somewhat unexpected. It was anticipated that such other variables as rank, active or retired status, and year of Vietnam tour would account for a portion of the variance in supportive orientation, but such was not the case. Though unexpected, the influence of these four characteristics may not be regarded as anomalous. The mystique attached to the West Point experience is legendary. Cadets endure an early and intense indoctrination into the "can do" ethos. Despite the quarter-

Table 4
Determinants of Overall Support for United States Efforts in Vietnam

Independent Variables	Controlling for	
	Source of Commission	Branch
Airborne Qualification	$F = 5.192*$	3.823*
	Source of Commission	Airborne Qualification
Branch	$F = 1.172$	1.219
	Branch	Airborne Qualification
Source of commission	$F = .918$	.963

Interactive Effects	
Airborne-Branch	$F = .253$
Airborne-Source	$F = 1.179$
Source-Branch	$F = .463$

*$P \leq .05$
$N = 108$

century of professional experience which West Point graduates have shared with their non-Academy counterparts, it appears that the earliest training experience produced an impact which for many is lasting.

Differences attributable to combat branch are also amenable to explanation. Although the Vietnam War was generally considered unconventional, it was least conventional from the standpoint of those trained in traditional armor tactics, which are more applicable to the north German plain or to a desert. That the war was to a great extent an infantryman's war is reflected in the above findings.

So, too, the airborne/non-airborne distinction has some plausible basis. It seems reasonable to suggest that a kind of esprit might exist among members of such a self-perceived elite which would lead them to be less self-critical. Whether individuals with such an outlook select themselves into airborne training or whether such training socializes participants into such an orientation remains an interesting question, but one which cannot be confronted here. As mentioned earlier, William Cockerham, in a study of this matter, concludes that action-oriented individuals select themselves into airborne training and bring their values and attitudes with them, as contrasted with the notion that the training is responsible for a change in their orientation.[2]

2. William Cockerham, "Selective Socialization: Airborne Training As Status Passage," *Journal of Political and Military Sociology*, 1 (1973), 215–229.

Appendix III

United States Army Commanding Generals In Vietnam

(January 1965 to December 1972)

(Listed under highest rank held as an operational commander in Vietnam. General officer operational command positions were: Commander, U.S. Military Assistance Command Vietnam (COMUSMACV); Deputy COMUSMACV; Chief of Staff USMACV; Commanding General (CG), Field Force or U.S. Corps, Deputy CG, Field Force or U.S. Corps; Chief of Staff, Field Force or U.S. Corps; CG Artillery, Field Force or U.S. Corps; Division Commander; Assistant Division Commander; CG Separate Brigade; Advisor Vietnamese Corps or equivalent position.)

Generals
Creighton W. Abrams
Andrew J. Goodpaster
William B. Rosson
William C. Westmoreland
Frederick W. Weyand

Lieutenant Generals
Arthur S. Collins, Jr.
Charles A. Corcoran
Michael S. Davison
Welborn G. Dolvin
Julian J. Ewell
John A. Heintges
Walter T. Kerwin, Jr.
Stanley R. Larsen
Bruce Palmer, Jr.
William R. Peers
Jonathan O. Seaman
Richard G. Stilwell
James W. Sutherland, Jr.
John L. Throckmorton
Melvin Zais

Major Generals
James L. Baldwin
Olinto A. Barsanti
Edward Bautz, Jr.
Charles P. Brown
William A. Burke
George W. Casey
Howard H. Cooksey
Donald H. Cowles
William E. De Pùy
George S. Eckhardt
George I. Forsythe
Marshall B. Garth
Charles M. Gettys
John H. Hay, Jr.
John J. Hennessey
James F. Hollingsworth
Harris W. Hollis
Harry W. O. Kinnard
Richard T. Knowles
Samuel W. Koster
Frederick J. Kroesen, Jr.
Fillmore K. Mearns

Albert E. Milloy
Hal D. McCown
John Norton
George G. O'Connor
Donn P. Pepke
George W. Putnam, Jr.
Lloyd B. Ramsey
Walter B. Richardson
Elvy B. Roberts
Joseph R. Russ
Charles P. Stone
Orwin C. Talbott
Thomas M. Tarpley
John C. F. Tillson, III
Elias C. Townsend
Jack J. Wagstaff
Glenn D. Walker
Keith L. Ware
Roderick Wetherill
Ellis W. Williamson
Gilbert H. Woodward
John MacN. Wright, Jr.

Brigadier Generals
Richard J. Allen
DeWitt C. Armstrong, III
Roy L. Atteberry, Jr.
John W. Barnes
William A. Becker
Warren K. Bennett
Sidney B. Berry
Edwin F. Black
George S. Blanchard
Linton S. Boatwright
Alexander R. Bolling, Jr.
Donnelly P. Bolton
William R. Bond
Thomas W. Bowen
Albert R. Brownfield, Jr.
Allen M. Burdett, Jr.
Jonathan R. Burton
Thomas J. Camp, Jr.
George G. Cantlay
Charles Cantrell

Lawrence H. Caruthers, Jr.
Carter W. Clarke, Jr.
Frank B. Clay
Wallace L. Clement
William S. Coleman
Robert E. Connor
Willis D. Crittenberger, Jr.
Hubert S. Cunningham
John H. Cushman
Franklin M. Davis, Jr.
Oscar E. Davis
Frederic E. Davison
John R. Deane, Jr.
Edward H. DeSaussure, Jr.
Wm. R. Desobry
Randolph C. Dickens
George W. Dickerson
John W. Donaldson
Donald D. Dunlop
Harold H. Dunwoody
Gordon J. Duquemin
Emil P. Eschenburg
Edward M. Flanagan, Jr.
Robert C. Forbes
Eugene P. Forrester
John F. Freund
William B. Fulton
James V. Galloway
William T. Gleason
Bertram K. Gorwitz
Michael J. L. Greene
Edward F. Gudgel, Jr.
Frank L. Gunn
Charles M. Hall
James F. Hamlet
Michael D. Healy
Davie S. Henderson
John Q. Henion
Don Rue Hickman
John G. Hill, Jr.
Robert C. Hixon
Burnside E. Huffman, Jr.
Arthur S. Hyman
Richard L. Irby

Albin F. Irzyk
Charles A. Jackson
Richard H. Johnson
James G. Kalergis
Maurice W. Kendall
Douglas Kinnard
William A. Knowlton
Robert J. Koch
William R. Kraft, Jr.
Richard M. Lee
John S. Lekson
Frank H. Linnell
Glen C. Long
Jack MacFarlane
Theodore C. Mataxis
Salve H. Matheson
Frank Meszar
Stewart C. Meyer
Charles McN. Mount, Jr.
Henry J. Muller, Jr.
Raymond P. Murphy
Robert C. McAlister
Dennis P. McAuliffe
Joseph C. McDonough
John R. McGiffert, III
Thomas J. McGuire, Jr.
Elmer R. Ochs
Willard Pearson

Allan G. Pixton
Edwin L. Powell, Jr.
Patrick W. Powers
Carleton Preer, Jr.
William O. Quirey
Francis J. Roberts
Bernard W. Rogers
Morgan G. Roseborough
Charles W. Ryder, Jr.
Frederick A. Schaefer, III
Leo H. Schweiter
Robert C. Shaw
William E. Shedd, III
Robert M. Shoemaker
Winant Sidle
Albert C. Smith
James C. Smith
Olin E. Smith
Paul F. Smith
Charles A. Smyroski
Charles R. Sniffin
John R. Thurman, III
James S. Timothy
George A. Wear
John G. Wheelock, III
Herbert E. Wolff
George H. Young, Jr.

Bibliography

The primary original sources used in this book were the responses to the September 1974 questionnaire. One hundred and seventy-three questionnaires were mailed. Completed questionnaires were received from 110 generals (two completed questionnaires arrived too late to be used in the data analysis) and letter responses from five others. Many of the questionnaires included written comments by the respondents; some wrote many pages.

In the summer of 1975 I conducted follow-through interviews with twenty of the respondents. Also in that summer I was able to research the unclassified files of the Current History Branch of the Army Military History Center in Washington.

From among the many public sources of information available on the Vietnam War that I examined, I found the following most useful.

Books

Ambrose, Stephen E. *Duty, Honor, Country*. Baltimore, Johns Hopkins Press, 1966.
Ambrose, Stephen E. and Barker, James A., Jr., eds. *The Military And American Society*. New York, The Free Press, 1972.
American Enterprise Institute. *Rational Debate Series—Vietnam Settlement: Why 1973, Not 1969?*. Washington D.C., 1973.
Asprey, Robert B. *War in the Shadows*. New York, Doubleday, 1975.

Barnet, Richard. "The Manipulation of Public Opinion," in *Roots of War*. New York, Atheneum, 1972.
Bletz, Donald F. *The Role of the Military Professional*. New York, Praeger, 1972.
Bradford, Zeb B., and Brawn, Frederic J. *The United States Army In Transition*. Beverly Hills, Sage, 1973.
Brandon, Henry. *Anatomy of Error*. Boston, Gambit, 1969.

Brodie, Bernard. *War and Politics*. New York, Macmillan, 1973.

Buhite, Russell, ed. *The Dynamics of World Power. A Documentary History of U.S. Foreign Policy 1945–1973*, 5 vols. Vol. 4, *The Far East*. New York, Chelsea House, 1973.

Bunting, Josiah. *The Lionheads*. New York, George Braziller, 1972.

Buttinger, Joseph. *Vietnam: A Dragon Embattled*. Vol. 1, *From Colonialism to the Vietnimh*. Vol. 2, *Vietnam at War*. New York, Praeger, 1967.

Cochran, Charles L. *Civil-Military Relations*. New York, The Free Press, 1974.

Collins, John M. *Grand Strategy*. Annapolis, Naval Institute Press, 1973.

Cooper, Chester. *The Lost Crusade*. New York, Dodd, Mead, 1970.

Corson, William R. *The Betrayal*. New York, Norton, 1968.

Corson, William R. *Consequences of Failure*. New York, Norton, 1974.

Critchfield, Richard. *The Long Charade: Political Subversion in the Vietnam War*. New York, Harcourt, Brace and World, 1968.

Duncanson, Dennis Jr. *Government and Revolution In Vietnam*. New York, Oxford University Press, 1968.

Ellis, Joseph J., and Moore, Robert. *School for Soldiers*. New York, Oxford University Press, 1974.

Ellsberg, Daniel. *Papers On the War*. New York, Simon and Schuster, 1972.

Epstein, Edward Jay. *News from Nowhere*. New York, Random House, 1973.

Falk, Richard A. *The Vietnam War and International Law*. 4 vols., Princeton, Princeton University Press, 1968, 1969, 1972.

Fall, Bernard B. *The Two Viet-Nams*. New York, Praeger, 1963.

Fitzgerald, Frances. *Fire in the Lake*. Boston, Little, Brown, 1972.

Furguson, Ernest B. *Westmoreland: The Inevitable General*. Boston, Little, Brown, 1968.

Galloway, K. Bruce, and Johnson, Robert Bowie. *West Point: America's Power Fraternity*. New York, Simon and Schuster, 1973.

Gallucci, Robert L. *Neither Peace nor Honor*. Baltimore, The Johns Hopkins University Press, 1975.

Giap, General Vo Nguyen. *People's War, People's Army*. New York, Praeger, 1962.

Goodman, Allan E. *Politics in War: The Bases of Political Community in South Vietnam*. Cambridge, Harvard University Press, 1973.

Goulding, Phil G. *Confirm Or Deny*. New York, Harper and Row, 1970.

Graff, Henry. *The Tuesday Cabinet: Deliberation and Decision on Peace and War under Lyndon B. Johnson.* Englewood Cliffs, N.J., Prentice Hall, 1970.

Griffith, Samuel B., II, Brig. Gen. USMC (Ret.). *Peking and People's Wars.* New York, Praeger, 1966.

Halberstam, David. *The Making of a Quagmire.* New York, Random House, 1964.

Halberstam, David. *The Best and the Brightest.* New York, Random House, 1972.

Hammer, Ellen J. *The Struggle for Indochina.* Stanford, Stanford University Press, 1954.

Harris, Louis. *The Anguish of Change.* New York, Norton, 1973.

Hauser, William L. *America's Army in Crisis.* Baltimore, The Johns Hopkins University Press, 1973.

Helmer, John. *Bringing the War Home.* New York, The Free Press, 1974.

Hersch, Seymour M. *Cover-Up.* New York, Random House, 1972.

Hilsman, Roger. *To Move a Nation.* New York, Doubleday, 1967.

Hilsman, Roger. "Two American Counterstrategies to Guerilla Warfare: The Case of Vietnam." *China in Crisis*, Vol. 2. Ed. Tang Tsou. Chicago, University of Chicago Press, 1968.

Ho, Ping-ti, and Tsou, Tang, eds. *China in Crisis*, Vol. 1. Chicago, University of Chicago Press, 1968.

Hoopes, Townsend. *The Limits of Intervention.* New York, David McKay, 1969.

Howard, Michael. *Studies in War and Peace.* New York, Viking Press, Compass Edition, 1972.

Isard, Walter. *Vietnam: Some Basic Issues and Alternatives.* Cambridge, Schenkman, 1969.

Janowitz, Morris. *The Professional Soldier.* New York, The Free Press, 1971.

Johnson, Chalmers. *Autopsy on People's War.* Berkeley, University of California Press, 1973.

Johnson, Lyndon Baines. *The Vantage Point.* New York, Holt, Rinehart, and Winston, 1971.

Joiner, Charles A. *The Politics of Massacre.* Philadelphia, Temple University Press, 1974.

Just, Ward. *Military Men.* New York, Knopf, 1970.

Kalb, Marvin, and Kalb, Bernard. *Kissinger.* Boston, Little, Brown, 1974.

Kalb, Marvin, and Abel, Elie. *Roots of Involvement*. New York, Norton, 1971.

Kearns, Doris. *Lyndon Johnson and the American Dream*. New York, Harper and Row, 1976.

King, Edward L. *The Death of the Army*. New York, Saturday Review Press, 1972.

Knightly, Philip. *The First Casualty*. New York, Harcourt Brace, Jovanovich, 1974.

Ky, Nguyen Cao. *Twenty Months and Twenty Days*. New York, Stein and Day, 1976.

Lansdale, Edward Geary. *In the Midst of Wars: An American Mission to Southeast Asia*. New York, Harper and Row, 1972.

Lefever, Ernest W. *TV and National Defense*. Boston, Va., Institute for American Strategy Press, 1974.

Levantrosser, William F. *Congress and the Citizen-Soldier*. Columbus, Ohio State University Press, 1967.

Lewallen, John. *Ecology of Devastation: Indochina*. Baltimore, Penguin Books, 1971.

Lifton, Robert Jay. *Home from the War*. New York, Simon and Schuster, 1973.

McAlister, J.T. *Vietnam; The Origins of Revolution*. New York, Alfred Knopf, 1969.

Mecklin, John. *Mission in Torment*. New York, Doubleday, 1965.

Mueller, John E. *War, Presidents and Public Opinion*. New York, Wiley, 1973.

Mylander, Maureen. *The Generals*. New York, Dial Press, 1974.

Oberdorfer, Don. *Tet!* New York, Doubleday, 1971.

O'Neill, Robert J. *General Giap*. New York, Praeger, 1969.

Petersen, Peter B. *Against the Tide*. New Rochelle, N.Y., Arlington House, 1974.

Pfeffer, Richard M. *No More Vietnams?* New York, Harper and Row, 1968.

Pike, Douglas. *Viet Cong*. Cambridge, M.I.T. Press, 1966.

Race, Jeffrey. *War Comes to Long An*. Berkeley, University of California Press, 1972.

Roosevelt, Elliott. *As He Saw It*. New York, Duell, 1946.

Rosenman, Samuel I. *The Public Papers and Addresses of Franklin D. Roosevelt*, Vol. 13. New York, Harper, 1944–45.

Samson, Robert L. *The Economics of Insurgency in the Mekong Delta of Vietnam*. Cambridge, Mass., MIT Press, 1970.
Sarkesian, Sam C. *The Professional Army Officer in a Changing Society*. Chicago, Nelson-Hall, 1975.
Schell, Jonathan. *The Village Of Ben Suc*. New York, Knopf, 1967.
Schlesinger, Arthur M., Jr. *The Bitter Heritage: Vietnam and American Democracy 1941–1966*. Boston, Houghton Mifflin, 1966.
Shaplen, Robert. *The Lost Revolution*. New York, Harper and Row, 1965.
Shaplen, Robert. *The Road from War: Vietnam 1965–1971*. New York, Harper and Row, 1971.
Stavins, Ralph; Barnet, Richard J.; and Raskin, Marcus G. *Washington Plans an Aggressive War*. New York, Random House, 1971.

Tanham, George K. *Communist Revolutionary Warfare*. New York, Praeger, 1961.
Taylor, Maxwell D. *Swords and Plowshares*. New York, Norton, 1972.
Taylor, Telford. *Nuremberg and Vietnam*. Chicago, Quadrangle Books, 1970.
Thompson, Robert. *No Exit from Vietnam*. New York, David McKay, 1970.
Trooboff, Peter D., ed. *Law and Responsibility in Warfare*. Chapel Hill, University of North Carolina Press, 1975.

Walt, Lewis W. *Strange War, Strange Strategy*. New York, Funk and Wagnalls, 1970.
Westmoreland, William C. *A Soldier Reports*. New York, Doubleday, 1976.

Zasloff, Joseph J., and Goodman, Allan E. *Indochina in Conflict*. Lexington, Heath, 1972.

Articles and Unpublished Papers

Bailey, George Arthur. "The Vietnam War According to Chet, David, Walter, Henry, Peter, Bob, Howard and Frank: A Content Analysis of Journalistic Performance by the Network Television Evening News Anchormen, 1965–1970." Unpublished Ph.D. Dissertation. U. of Wisconsin, January 1974.
Ball, George. "The Lessons of Vietnam: Have We Learned or Only Failed?" *New York Times Magazine*, April 1, 1973.
Buchan, Alastair. "The Indochina War and World Politics." *Foreign Affairs*, 53, (1975), 638-650.

Clifford, Clark M. "A Viet Nam Reappraisal: The Personal History of One
    Man's View and How It Evolved." *Foreign Affairs*, 47 (1969)
    601–622.
Cockerham, William C. "Selective Socialization: Airborne Training as a
    Status Passage." *Journal of Political and Military Sociology*, 1
    (1973), 215–229.

Gelb, Leslie H. "Vietnam: The System Worked." *Foreign Policy*, 3
    (1971), 140–167.
Geyelin, Philip. "The Role of the Press in an Open Society." *Naval War
    College Review*, 27 (1975), 3–7.
Goodnow, Chandler, et al. "News Coverage of the Tet Offensive." Un-
    published Student Research Paper, U.S. Army War College, Car-
    lisle Barracks, Pa., 1969.
Grinter, Lawrence E. "Bargaining Between Saigon and Washington: Di-
    lemmas of Linkage Politics During War." *ORBIS*, 18 (1974),
    837–867.

Halberstam, David. "The Power and the Profits," Part II. *Atlantic* (Feb-
    ruary 1976), pp. 52–91.
Halperin, Morton H. "War Termination as a Problem in Civil-Military
    Relations." *Annals of the American Academy of Political and
    Social Science*, 392 (1970), 86–95.

Kahin, George McT. "The Pentagon Papers: A Critical Evaluation."
    American Political Science Review, 69 (1975), 675–684.
Kissinger, Henry. "Vietnam: The End of the War." *Survival*, 17 (1975),
    183–186.
Krepon, Michael. "Weapons Potentially Inhumane: The Case of Cluster
    Bombs." *Foreign Affairs*, 57 (1974), 595–611.

Lynch, Marianne. *The Soviet Union and Vietnam*. A Monograph on
    National Security Affairs, Brown University, July 1975.

Matthews, Lloyd J., Col., U.S. Army. "Farewell the Tranquil Mind: Se-
    curity and Stability in the Post-Vietnam Era." *Parameters,
    Journal of the U.S. Army War College*, 5 (1976), 2–13.
Midgail, Carl J. "A Perspective of the Military and the Media." *Naval
    War College Review*, 28 (1976), 2–9.

Parker, Maynard. "Vietnam: The War That Won't End." *Foreign Affairs*,
    53 (1975), 352–374.
Probert, John R. "The Reserves and National Guard: Their Changing

Role in National Defense." *Naval War College Review*, 24 (1972), 66–75.

Ridgway, Matthew B. "Indochina: Disengaging." *Foreign Affairs*, 49 (1971), 583–592.

Russett, Bruce M. "Political Perspectives of U.S. Military and Business Elites." *Armed Forces and Society*, 1 (1974), 79–108.

Savage, Paul L., and Richard A. Gabriel. "Beyond Vietnam: Cohesion and Disintegration in the American Army." Paper presented at the 16th annual convention of the International Studies Association, Washington, D.C., February 1975.

Shaplen, Robert. "Southeast Asia—Before and After." *Foreign Affairs*, 53 (1975), 533–557.

Shoup, David. "The New American Militarism." *Atlantic* (April 1969), 51–56.

Siracusa, Joseph M. "The United States, Vietnam, and the Cold War: A Reappraisal." *Journal of Southeast Asian Studies*, Singapore, 5 (1974), 82–101.

Szulc, Tad. "Behind the Vietnam Cease-Fire Agreement." *Foreign Policy*, 15 (1974), 21–69.

Thomson, James C., Jr. "How Could Vietnam Happen? An Autopsy." *Atlantic* (April 1968), 47–53.

U'ren, Richard H. "West Point: Cadets, Codes and Careers." *Society*, 12 (1975), 23–29, 36.

Verba, Sidney, et al. "Public Opinion and the War in Vietnam." *American Political Science Review*, 61 (1967), 317–333.

Volgy, Thomas. *What Have We Done? An Examination of Some Scholarly Literature on the Vietnamese Conflict*. Tucson, Institute of Government Research, University of Arizona (1973).

Weil, Herman M. "Can Bureaucrats Be Rational Actors? Foreign Policy Decision-Making in North Vietnam." *International Studies Quarterly*, 19 (1975), 432–468.

Westerfield, H. Bradford. "What Use Are Three Versions of the Pentagon Papers?" *American Political Science Review*, 69 (1975), 685–696.

Westmoreland, William C. "Westmoreland in Vietnam: Pulverizing the 'Boulder'." *Army*, 26 (1976), 36–44.

Witcover, Jules, et al. "Where Washington Reporting Failed." *Columbia Journalism Review*, 9 (1970–71), 7–12.

Public Documents

Central Office for South Vietnam. "Resolution No. 9," July 1969.

Collins, James Lawton, Jr. *The Development and Training of the South Vietnamese Army*. Vietnam Studies. Washington, Government Printing Office, 1975.

Dunn, Carroll H. *Base Development in South Vietnam 1965–1970*. Vietnam Studies. Washington, Government Printing Office, 1972.

Eckhardt, George S. *Command and Control 1950–1969*. Vietnam Studies. Washington, Government Printing Office, 1974.

Elliott, David W. P., and W. A. Stewart. "Pacification and the Viet Cong System in Dinh Tuong: 1966–1967." RAND Corporation RM-5-88-ISA/ARPA, January 1969.

Ewell, Julian E., and Ira A. Hunt, Jr. *Sharpening the Combat Edge: The Use of Analysis to Reinforce Military Judgment*. Vietnam Studies. Washington, Government Printing Office, 1974.

Fulton, William B. *Riverine Operations 1966–1969*. Vietnam Studies. Washington, Government Printing Office, 1973.

Gavin, James M. Testimony Before Senate Committee on Foreign Relations, 2nd Session 1966. *Hearings: Supplemental Foreign Assistance*. Washington, Government Printing Office, 1966.

Gurtov, Melvin. and Kellen Konrad. *Vietnam: Lessons and Mislessons*. Santa Monica, California, RAND, 1969.

Hay, John H., Jr. *Tactical and Materiel Innovations*. Vietnam Studies. Washington, Government Printing Office, 1974.

Heiser, Joseph M., Jr. *Logistic Support*. Vietnam Studies. Washington, Government Printing Office, 1974.

Kaplan, Morton, et al. *Vietnam Settlement: Why 1973, Not 1969?* Washington, American Enterprise Institute for Public Policy Research, 1973.

Komer, R. W. *Bureaucracy Does Its Thing*. Santa Monica, California, RAND, 1972.

———. "Impact of Pacification on Insurgency in South Vietnam," RAND P4443, August 1970.

Larsen, Stanley R., and James Lawton, Jr. *Allied Participation in Vietnam*. Vietnam Studies. Washington, Government Printing Office, 1975.

McChristian, Joseph A. *The Role of Military Intelligence, 1965–1967*. Vietnam Studies. Washington, Government Printing Office, 1974.
Military Assistance Command, Vietnam. *Hamlet Evaluation System*, June 1969.

Nalty, Bernard C. *Air Power and the Fight for Khe Sanh*. Washington, Government Printing Office, 1973.

Palmer, Dave Richard. *The War in Vietnam, 1954–1968*. West Point, N.Y., U.S. Military Academy, 1969.
Pauker, Guy J. *An Essay on Vietnamization*, report prepared for the Advanced Research Projects Agency. Santa Monica, California, RAND, 1971.
Prugh, George S. *Law at War: Vietnam 1964–1973*. Vietnam Studies. Washington, Government Printing Office, 1975.

Rockett, Frederick C., and A. A. Berle. *RVNAF Effectiveness Evaluation*. Washington, Simulmatics Corporation, 1967.
Rogers, Bernard W. *Cedar Falls—Junction City: A Turning Point*. Vietnam Studies. Washington, Government Printing Office, 1974.

Taylor, Leonard B. *Financial Management of the Vietnam Conflict 1962–1972*. Vietnam Studies. Washington, Government Printing Office, 1974.
Tolson, John J. *Airmobility 1961–1971*. Vietnam Studies. Washington, Government Printing Office, 1973.

U.S. Army War College. *Leadership for the 1970's*. Washington, Government Printing Office, 1973.
———. *Study on Military Professionalism*. Carlisle Barracks, Pa., 1970.
U.S. 91st Congress, 2nd Session. Senate Committee on Foreign Relations. *Vietnam Policy and Prospects, 1970: Civil Operations and Rural Development Support Program: Hearings*. Washington, Government Printing Office, 1970.
U.S. 91st Congress, 2nd Session. Senate Committee on Foreign Relations. *Moral and Military Aspects of the War in Southeast Asia: Hearings*. Washington, Government Printing Office, 1970.
U.S. Department of the Army. *Report of the Department of the Army: Review of the Preliminary Investigations into the My Lai Incident*, Vol. 1. Washington, Government Printing Office, 1970.
U.S. Department of Defense. *The Pentagon Papers*. Gravel Edition, 5 vols., Boston, Beacon Press, 1971.

U.S. Joint Chiefs of Staff. *Dictionary of United States Terms for Joint Usage*. Washington, Government Printing Office, 1968.
U.S. Senate Committee on Foreign Relations. *Background Information Relating to Southeast Asia and Vietnam*. 7th revised ed., Washington, Government Printing Office, 1974.

Westmoreland, W. C. *Report on Operations in South Vietnam January 1964–June 1968*. Washington, Government Printing Office, 1969.

Index

About the Author

Douglas Kinnard graduated from West Point on June 6, 1944. He was in combat in Europe in World War II, the Korean War, and twice in the Vietnam War. He was the third member of his West Point class to become a general and retired voluntarily in 1970 to pursue an academic career, receiving the Ph.D. from Princeton in 1973. He subsequently joined the faculty of the University of Vermont and became Professor Emeritus of Political Science in 1984. From 1983 to 1984 he was Chief of Military History, US Army. He is now writing full-time and lives in Lexington, Virginia.